JUDGMENT CALLS IN RESEARCH

Studying Organizations:
Innovations in Methodology

PROJECT ON INNOVATIONS IN METHODOLOGY
FOR STUDYING ORGANIZATIONS

Project Planning Committee

Thomas J. Bouchard, *University of Minnesota*
Joel T. Campbell, *Educational Testing Service*
David L. DeVries, *Center for Creative Leadership*
J. Richard Hackman (Chair), *Yale University*
Joseph L. Moses, *American Telephone and Telegraph Company*
Barry M. Staw, *University of California, Berkeley*
Victor H. Vroom, *Yale University*
Karl E. Weick, *Cornell University*

Project Sponsorship and Administration

The volumes in this series (listed above) are among the products of a multi-year project on innovations in methodology for organizational research, sponsored by Division 14 (Industrial and Organizational Psychology) of the American Psychological Association.

Support for the project was provided jointly by the Organizational Effectiveness Research Program of the Office of Naval Research (Bert T. King, Scientific Officer), and by the School Management and Organizational Studies Unit of the National Institute of Education (Fritz Mulhauser, Scientific Officer). The central office of the American Psychological Association contributed its services for the management of project finances.

Technical and administrative support for the project was provided by the Center for Creative Leadership (Greensboro, NC) under the direction of David L. DeVries and Ann M. Morrison.

JUDGMENT CALLS IN RESEARCH

by
Joseph E. McGrath, Joanne Martin,
and **Richard A. Kulka**

Published in cooperation with Division 14 of the
AMERICAN PSYCHOLOGICAL ASSOCIATION

SAGE PUBLICATIONS
Beverly Hills / London / New Delhi

Portions of this book appeared in *American Behavioral Scientist*
(Volume 25, Number 2, November/December 1981), © 1981 by Sage
Publications, Inc.

For information address:

SAGE Publications, Inc.
275 South Beverly Drive
Beverly Hills, California 90212

SAGE Publications India Pvt. Ltd.
C-236 Defence Colony
New Delhi 110 024, India

SAGE Publications Ltd
28 Banner Street
London EC1Y 8QE, England

Printed in the United States of America

Library of Congress Cataloging in Publication Data

McGrath, Joseph Edward, 1927-
    Judgment calls in research.

    (Studying organizations : innovations in methodology ;
v. 2)
    "Published in cooperation with Division 14 of the
American Psychological Association."
    Bibliography: p.
    1. Social sciences—Research—Addresses, essays,
lectures. I. Martin, Joanne Mitchell. II. Kulka,
Richard A. III. American Psychological Association.
Division of Industrial-Organizational Psychology.
IV. Title. V. Series.
H62.M336 1982   300'.72   82-16732
ISBN 0-8039-1873-9
ISBN 0-8039-1874-7 (pbk.)

SECOND PRINTING, 1983

Contents

Preface

There has been increasing interest in recent years, both in academia and in society at large, in how—and how well—organizations function. Educational, human service, political, and work organizations all have come under close scrutiny by those who manage them, those who work in them, and those who are served by them.

The questions that have been raised are important ones. How, for example, can organizations become leaner (and, in many cases, smaller) as the birthrate and the rate of economic growth decline? Is there a trade-off between organizational productivity and the quality of life at work? Or can life at work and productivity be simultaneously improved? What changes in organizational practices are required to increase the career mobility of traditionally disadvantaged groups in society? How are we to understand the apparent asynchrony between the goals of educational organizations and the requirements of work organizations? How can public services be provided more responsively and with greater cost effectiveness? What new and nondiscriminatory devices can be developed to test, assess, and place people in schools and in industry? The list goes on, and it is long.

Unfortunately, there is reason for concern about our capability to build a systematic base of knowledge that can be used to deal with questions such as these. Available strategies for studying organizations have emerged more or less independently from a variety of disciplines, ranging from anthropology, sociology, and political science to educational, industrial, and organizational psychology. But none of these disciplines appears to be on the verge of generating the kind of knowledge about organizations that will be required to understand them in their full richness and complexity.

Why not? Part of the problem may have to do with the *restrictiveness* of discipline-based research—that is, the tendency of academic disciplines to support specific and focused research paradigms, and to foster intense but narrow study of particular and well-defined research "topics." Another possibility, however, is that the *methodologies* used in research on organizations have been far too limited and conventional.

In general, the methods used in studying organizations have been imported from one or another of the academic disciplines. And while these methods may be fully appropriate for the particular research problems and paradigms that are dominant in the disciplines from which they come, they also may blind those who use them to potentially significant new findings and insights about how organizations operate.

Because the need for higher quality organizational research is pressing, now may be the time to try to break through the constraints of traditional methodologies and seek new approaches to organizational research. This was the thinking of the Executive Committee of Division 14 (Industrial and Organizational Psychology) of the American Psychological Association when, a few years ago, it initiated a project intended to foster innovations in methodology for organizational research. A planning committee was appointed, and support was obtained from the Office of Naval Research and the National Institute of Education. Eighteen scholars were recruited from a variety of disciplines and formed into six working groups to review the state of organizational research methodologies, and to seek innovative approaches to understanding organizations. A three-day conference was held at the

Center for Creative Leadership, at which about sixty organizational researchers (representing a variety of disciplinary orientations, and from applied as well as academic settings) reviewed the findings and proposals of the six working groups. The working groups then revised their materials based on the reactions of conference participants, and the six monographs in this series are the result.

The content of the six monographs is wide ranging, from new quantitative techniques for analyzing data to alternative ways of gathering and using qualitative data about organizations. From "judgment calls" in designing research on organizations, to ways of doing research that encourage the *implementation* of the research findings. From innovative ways of formulating research questions about organizations to new strategies for cumulating research findings across studies.

This monograph focuses specifically on better ways of making "judgment calls" in methodological decision making. The monograph calls into question traditional, rational models for making methodological decisions in organizational research. Instead, methodological decisions are viewed as involving trade-offs among competing alternatives, none of which may be optimal. Throughout, the discrepancies between what one *should* do (according to methodology textbooks) and what first-rate researchers *actually* do are highlighted, and some ideas for dealing creatively with the dilemmas of methodological decision making in organizational research are presented.

The aspiration of the numerous people who contributed their time and talent to the innovations project (they are listed facing the title page) is that readers of this monograph—and of its companions in the series—will discover here some ideas about methods that can be used to benefit both the quality and the usefulness of their own research on organizations.

—J. Richard Hackman
Series Editor

Acknowledgments

We would like to thank the coordinating committee, especially J. Richard Hackman and Barry Staw, who provided crucial and appropriate leadership in a timely fashion. We acknowledge and appreciate the many forms of help given by members of the Center for Creative Leadership staff, especially David DeVries, Ann Morrison, Mary Ellen Kranz, Bill Jennings, and Jane Swanson. We also appreciate the contributions of the members of five other workshops of the conference.

We especially appreciate the contributions of the workshop participants, who listened patiently, queried wisely, and helped us strubble with very difficult material.

We would also like to thank Sage Publications for allowing us to publish an earlier draft of this manuscript in *American Behavioral Scientist,* Volume 25, Number 2, November/December 1981.

J.E.M.
J. M.
R.A.K.

Introduction

Joseph E. McGrath

□ "Judgment calls" is a term borrowed from baseball. There, it refers to all of those decisions (some big, some small, but all necessary and consequential) that must be made without the benefit of a fixed, "objective" rule that one can apply, with precision, like a template or a pair of calipers. It includes such crucial decisions as: Was that pitch in the strike zone? Did the batter hold up the swing, or follow through so far that it constitutes a strike? Did the shortstop control the ball long enough (before dropping it) for the runner to be called out?

In baseball, such judgment calls accumulate in their effects; and, indeed, they quite literally determine the outcome of most games. Similarly, in research, there are many crucial decisions that must be made without the benefit of a hard and fast, "objective" rule, or even a good algorithm or general rule of thumb. And, as in baseball, the cumulative results of such judgment calls often determine the outcome of research. Consideration of such judgment calls—the most difficult, or at least the most ambiguous, decisions needed in the planning and conduct of research in behavioral and social science—is the focus of this volume.

In the various chapters of this volume, we try to deal with choices in the research process at several different levels (e.g., strategy, design, measurement), from several different perspectives (e.g., traditional rational or structured models versus much more chaotic, dynamic ones), and by means of several different forms of evidence (logical argument, survey results, experiential anecdotes). We attempt to provide an analytic treatment of key decisions in the research process: the alternatives from among which the researcher may choose; the circumstances that constrain, or at least influence, such choices; and the consequences—including intended and unintended effects and opportunity costs—that ensue from those choices. But, of course, we cannot do so completely because our capabilities, as well as our space in this volume, are limited.

We do *not* attempt to provide a set of rules, or algorithms, to handle such judgment calls in fixed and systematic ways. It is our shared view—reflected in many passages of several chapters within this volume—that one loses a great deal when one attempts to fashion sound research entirely on the basis of general decision rules routinely applied. Rather, we believe one should retain a very important place for the judgments of the skilled researcher who, at best, will be sensitive to nuances of both the substantive setting and the research impedimenta; and who, at least, can observe when something stunningly unexpected occurs, and can perhaps stop the churning of the research machine long enough to take a look at it. We suggest, therefore, that a set of rules to replace judgment calls not only would be difficult to fashion, but also would be dysfunctional if we had them. It is good, we argue, to have and to recognize, explicitly, a set of crucial judgment calls within the research process, at which junctures the investigators' unique skills/resources/purposes can be brought to bear. We do, however, offer another kind of "rule"; but that will be discussed after first noting briefly the contents of each of the chapters.

In Chapter 1, Martin takes issue with the traditional (textbook) model that pictures the research process as a neat and orderly series of logically directed steps. She proposes a model for research decisions analogous to Cohen, March, and Olsen's (1972) "garbage can" model of decision making in organizations. Four streams of factors swirl together in that garbage can—theories, methods, resources, and solutions. Each constrains and is constrained by the others, and each potentially serves as "forcing function" to trigger and direct the research process.

Kulka documents many of the points made in Martin's chapter and in the later chapter by McGrath, by presenting a series of vignettes recounting key research decisions. These vignettes are drawn from interviews and printed accounts in which experienced behavioral science researchers discuss key decisions—judgment calls—in their own past research projects. These accounts would seem to support Martin's contention that the research process, in practice, is a far less orderly stream of behavior and judgments than is the research process as presented in most textbooks on methodology, not to mention the method section of most research articles.

McGrath tries to show how even the idealized, or traditional, or rational-normative model has serious flaws. He argues that research involves a series of dilemmas—choices among mutually conflicting desiderata—and that those dilemmas can neither be "solved" nor avoided. Thus, in principle, all research methods are seriously flawed—though each is flawed differently. Multiple studies involving diverse methods are not just desirable, but rather a sine qua non for the knowledge accrual process.

While we eschewed the idea of setting forth a batch of rules for making specific research decisions, our explorations of these matters led us to formulate a set of "rules" of another genre. Rather than proposing a set of rules for deciding specific research issues, we offer—in our jointly authored, fourth chapter in this volume—a set of rules for avoiding some of the most seductive and deadly pitfalls in the research process. Thus, for example, while we cannot advise a researcher what he or she ought to do "next" even if given all pertinent details of the problem and research situation, we can offer some advice about what he or she *ought not* to do next. A set of such quasi-rules is the core of the jointly authored chapter that concludes the substantive material of this volume. The volume closes with a capstone piece by Barry Staw, who served as the "shepherd" of the workshop group, that puts the material of this volume into a broader research perspective.

The reader should be warned that what we offer here is likely to seem, at first sight, a negative and even cynical view of research methodology—of future innovations as well as of the current state of the art. We present the research process as being horrendously complex, and indeed, as being quite intractible in places. We concede that what we offer is a skeptical view. We believe it is a realistic view. We see nothing to be gained by pretending that our tools and tactics can do what they cannot. But we do not believe that our perspective need be a cynical one, nor do we draw from it cynical or nihilistic conclusions about the future of research in our field. Rather, we draw what might be regarded as cautiously optimistic conclusions. In these chapters we have tried to make explicit the complexity and the intractibility of some aspects of the research process. We are firm in our belief that, by doing so, we do not *cause* the research process to become more complex or more intractible, but rather merely clarify what is already the case. To explicate its difficulties does not make research more difficult, or even more frustrating, to perform. Indeed, it may make research easier and more rewarding. If the researcher can better understand the nature of the task and the limits of success on it, expectations are thereby much less likely to be set far out of line with even the best possible results. However difficult the problem, we would hold, it is always better to understand its difficulty than not to. In research as in other decision-making areas, planned ignorance is never a virtue.

REFERENCE

COHEN, D., J. G. MARCH, and J. P. OLSEN (1972) "A garbage can model of organizational choice." Administrative Science Quarterly 17: 1-25.

1

A Garbage Can Model of the Research Process

Joanne Martin

☐ Journal articles and the more conventional methodological textbooks present a rational model of the process of doing research. Consider the headings in a typical journal article: survey of literature, hypotheses, methods, results, and discussion. Many methodological textbooks structure the presentation of the research process in a similar fashion. For example, one text lists chapters on the selection and formulation of a research problem, research design, general problems in measurement, data collection, analysis, and interpretation (Selltiz et al., 1959).

The steps in the research process, implied by the order of these journal headings and chapter titles, are labeled in this chapter as the "rational model." In its simplest form, that model has four steps:

(1) formulate a theoretical problem;
(2) select appropriate research method(s); design and conduct study;

Author's Note: This article has grown out of discussions with Barry Staw, Richard Kulka, Melanie E. Powers, Eugene Webb, Morgan McCall, and James G. March. I am grateful for their helpful comments.

(3) analyze and interpret results; and
(4) use results to confirm/deny theory.

Each of these steps is discussed briefly below.

The rational model begins with the formulation of the research problem. The focus of this chapter is on basic research and thus the problem should be theoretical. According to the rational model, the researcher should critically review the literature on a given topic in order to find an important issue that previous research has failed to resolve successfully. Typically, the literature on a narrowly specialized topic is reviewed and hypotheses are derived in an overtly deductive fashion.

The second step in the rational model is to select a method or methods to study the chosen theoretical problem. According to the rational model, the nature of the theoretical problem should determine the choice of the most appropriate research method. An even more ideal solution would be triangulation, the use of several different methods to address the same theoretical questions (e.g., Campbell and Fiske, 1959). Triangulation has many well-known advantages. For example, it may help the researcher detect relationships that might otherwise have been unsuspected. For reasons such as this, triangulation is often recommended as the most preferred methodological strategy (e.g., Runkel and McGrath, 1972; Crano and Brewer, 1973).

According to the rational model, after selecting a method or methods and designing the study, the researcher collects and analyzes the data. The distinguishing feature of this rational model is the sequential structure of the research process. In the final step of the rational model, the researcher uses the results of the study to confirm and/or revise the theory. This last step, from results back to theory, makes the rational model cyclical as well as sequential.

This rational model is the most frequently cited normative approach to the research process. The rational model has a logical justification. It is an effective structure for presenting research findings. It is perhaps an idealized guide to how research ought to be conducted. The rational model does not attempt to provide an accurate description of the process whereby research *actually* is conducted. At the present time, to my knowledge, a commonly accepted descriptive model of the research process is not available.

RULES OF THUMB AND RESEARCH "STREET SMARTS"

Students are particularly aware of how useful it would be to have a model that accurately describes the actual process of conducting research. Students trying to learn how to do research are constantly faced with gaps between the rational model of many of their texts and teachers and the realities of how research actually is conducted. They must learn the "street smarts" of the research process, the rules of thumb that guide practical research decisions. Many students whose classes and textbooks are restricted to the rational approach are forced to learn about the inaccuracies of the rational model in a haphazard fashion. They decipher rules of thumb from throwaway lines in conversations with faculty, asides in methodology textbooks, and embarrassed footnotes in journal articles.

Other students learn about the inaccuracies of the rational model in a less haphazard fashion. They are exposed to a more realistic description of the process of conducting research in their methodology courses or in published sources (e.g., Campbell and Cook, 1979; Ellsworth, 1977; Webb and Ellsworth, 1975). These latter sources, however, have as their objective the improvement of the quality of research, rather than the provision of a theoretical model that describes the process whereby research decisions are actually made. The objective of this chapter is to provide such a realistic descriptive model of the research process.

Although this objective is theoretical, such a model might be of practical use to teachers and students of methodology. It should be less useful to an experienced researcher because, if such a model accurately reflects the reality of the research process, it should contain few new insights not already learned by experience. Some implications of the model concerning the state of knowledge in the field, however, may be surprising even to experienced researchers. Before presenting these implications, the descriptive model itself must be described.

RELEVANCE OF MODELS OF ORGANIZATIONAL DECISION MAKING

Although a theoretical model of the actual process of conducting research is not currently available, some philosophers and historians of science, and sociologists of knowledge, address aspects of this topic (e.g., Berger and Luckmann, 1966; Kuhn, 1970; Stark, 1967). The research process can be conceptualized as a series of decisions about what topic to study, what methodology to use, and so forth. When the research process is conceptualized in this way, the relevance of models of organizational decision making becomes clear.

Most of the organizational models of decision making make conventional, normative, rational assumptions about choice procedures. According to such theories, "choice opportunities lead first to the generation of decision alternatives, then to an examination of their consequences, then to an evaluation of those consequences in terms of objectives, and finally to a decision" (Cohen et al., 1972: 2). In its emphasis on rational criteria for making choices, and on the appropriate sequence of steps in the choice process, this rational model of decision making in organizational contexts bears a strong resemblance to the rational model of the research process. There is considerable evidence that this rational model does not accurately represent the way organizational decisions actually get made (e.g., Allison, 1969; Lindblom, 1965; March and Simon, 1958).

INTRODUCING THE GARBAGE CAN MODEL

March and his colleagues propose an alternative model of organizational decision making (Cohen et al., 1972; March and Olsen, 1976). According to this latter model, the process of decision making is conceptualized as a garbage can. As members of the organization generate problems and solutions, they dump these into the garbage can. Thus, an organization is seen as "a collection of choices looking for problems, issues and feelings looking for decision situations in which they might be aired, solutions looking for issues to which they might be the answer, and decision makers looking for work" (Cohen et al., 1972: 2). In the garbage can model four variables or "streams" circulate in a kind of Brownian movement in a fixed decision space, that decision space being the garbage can and those four variables being problems, decision participants, choice oppor- tunities, and solutions. The garbage can is more of a metaphor than a systematic theory. It is not even a model, in the technical sense of this term, although a computer simulation model of it has been built (see Cohen et al., 1972).

March and his colleagues propose that the garbage can model should be a particularly accurate description of the process of making decisions in an organized anarchy. Organ- ized anarchies are decision situations or organizations that are characterized by inconsistent and ill-defined preferences, un- clear technology, and fluid participation in the decision- making process.

The research process in the field (or in any subfield) of the social sciences has many of the attributes of activity in an organized anarchy. Consider the example of the field of psy- chology taken as a whole. First, preferences are obviously problematic. It is certainly more accurate to describe the field as a loose collection of ideas, rather than as a coherent structure having a shared intellectual paradigm (Kuhn, 1970). Second, the technologies that are used to conduct psychological research are flawed and not fully understood. Indeed, many of them are adopted from other disciplines or adapted to fit the needs of the moment. Third, participation in the research process is obviously fluid. Some researchers early in their careers publish a single study and are never heard from again. Others fade from view as soon as they get tenure, while still others provide an exemplary model of late-career productivity.

These examples support the argument for the relevance of the garbage can model to the research process. The field of organizational research has many of the attributes of an organized anarchy. If the garbage can model is relevant to the process of making research decisions in such fields, it is useful to define that model in some detail, as is done below.

The garbage can model was originally developed to explain decision processes in an organizational context, such as that provided by an organized anarchy. Before the relevance of this model in the research context can be fully explored, some specifications of the definitions of the four variables of the model are helpful. The organizational version of the garbage can model includes problems, decision participants, choice opportunities, and solutions. The garbage can model of the research process is concerned with problems that are theoretical, resources available to the research participants, choice opportunities as they refer to selection of methodology, and solutions that are the results of the research process itself. Each of these variables is defined more fully below.

THEORETICAL PROBLEMS

Whereas organizational problems are usually practical issues that suffer from a lack of resolution, because the focus of this chapter is on basic research, the problems of interest are theoretical in nature. In some cases these problems will be specified as hypotheses, while in other cases only a general topic of theoretical interest will be defined.

This definition does not deny the fact that researchers often select research problems for nontheoretical reasons and only afterwards go to the theoretical literature to seek a justification for making this particular problem the subject of their investigation. This garbage can model of the research process examines those nontheoretical reasons for the choice of a theoretical problem that involve the other variables in the garbage can model. Some nontheoretical causes for problem selection, however, are beyond the scope of the model. These include personal concerns of the researcher, historical considerations, and the socio-political-economic factors that are the focus of the fields of the sociology of knowledge, philosophy and history of science, and the like.

This presentation of the garbage can model does assume that nontheoretical reasons for the selection of a research problem can be treated separately from the theoretical justification for the selection of that problem. Some philosophers of science take the position that this assumption is unwarranted, that historical, personal, and socio-political-economic concerns cannot be distinguished from the theoretical justification for studying a particular problem (see Feyerabend, 1975).

RESOURCES

In the organizational version of the garbage can model the second variable is labeled "decision participants." These are the individuals who participate in a given decision situation. In the research process, this second variable is more accurately labeled "resources." The key issue is not simply who participates in a given research process. The issue of participation is determined by what resources a given research project requires.

The project may require resources from an individual research, such as abilities. For example, a particular methodological skill or simply raw intelligence may be needed. Other essential resources may include money or financial contributions, such as a subject pool or access to a field site. Rather than considering the different types of resources separately, the garbage can model of the research process includes resource availability as a single variable.

METHOD(S)

In the organizational version of the garbage can model, the third variable is a "choice opportunity." This is defined as an occasion "when an organization is expected to produce a behavior that can be called a decision" (March and Olsen, 1976: 26-27). There is no exact parallel for a choice opportunity in the research process, since researchers are by definition expected to produce research continuously. Thus, choice opportunities must and do constantly occur. Indeed, choice opportunities often merge with each other.

A more precise parallel to a choice opportunity is the point at which a researcher selects a method or methods. This is a choice, albeit a choice that can be influenced by many factors. Unlike the ongoing process of research, the choice of a method is a detectable decision. One can define the point at which this decision has been made. In this chapter, the method(s) variable includes both the choice of data collection mode(s) and data analytic procedure(s).

SOLUTIONS

Whereas "solutions" in organizational contexts are answers to problems, solutions in the research context require a more complex definition. In the latter context, solutions have two components: the empirical results of a given data collection effort and the theoretical interpretations given to those results. Providing that the data have been properly analyzed, the empirical content of those results is unlikely to change, while the interpretation of those results may vary considerably.

The definitions above specify the four variables or "streams" of the garbage can model of the research process: theoretical problems, resources, methodological choices, and solutions. Each of these variables can influence or not influence any of the others. In the next section of this chapter, the implications of this garbage can model of the research process are explored to see if this model is in fact more accurate than the rational model in describing the process of conducting organizational research.

THE GAP BETWEEN RATIONAL RHETORIC AND GARBAGE CAN REALITY

This section presents propositions derived from a pure form of the rational model, labeled "myths," and counterexamples derived from the garbage can model of the research process. Because the rational model is normative, it serves as an idealized standard against which actual performance can be measured. Obviously, researchers know that the myths described below represent idealized standards rather than accurate descriptions of the research process. These myths, then, are not to be seen as cherished truths about to be debunked. Instead, they are intended as springboards for an elaboration of the garbage can model.

Myth #1: Resources Are Important Only as an Enabling Condition of the Research Process. The rational model, as defined above, either excludes mention of resources or discusses resources only as enabling factors that must be present before the desired study can be conducted. The rational model assigns a passive role to resources.

The garbage can model allows resources to function actively, as a determining factor in the selection of a theoretical problem, the choice of a method, and even the interpretation of a solution. Each of these possibilities is discussed below.

Resource availability may influence the choice of a theoretical problem (e.g., Webb and Ellsworth, 1975). Indeed, government agencies providing funding and organizations providing site access deliberately attempt to influence researchers' theoretical focuses. For example, several years ago the National Institute of Mental Health (NIMH) issued research funding guidelines that included an interest in studies of the effects of minority status on mental health. This influenced some mental health researchers whose interest in minority issues had not heretofore been evident. It also encouraged some researchers who customarily focused on minority issues to develop an interest in mental health research.

In addition to affecting choice of theoretical problem, limitations in the resources available can affect the choice of a methodology (see Webb et al., 1972). Many of these limitations are caused by the individual researcher's abilities or personal preferences. Limited abilities are often the result of overly specialized training. For example, all too many researchers have been adequately trained in only one methodology. Not surprisingly, when faced with a choice, the researcher will select that particular methodology, irrespective of the nature of the theoretical problem he or she wishes to address.

Availability of resources on the organizational, rather than on the individual, level can generate reasons for the selection of a particular methodology. For example, the Survey Research Center (SRC) at the University of Michigan has an extraordinarily well-tooled "machine," consisting of people, techniques, and computers ready to design, administer, and analyze data from large-scale surveys. Irrespective of the type of theoretical problem the SRC researcher wants to address, there is, no doubt, some tacit pressure, due to the presence of these resources, to use survey methodology. As these examples indicate, the availability of resources, as determined by the capabilities and preferences of individuals and organizations, may influence the choice of a research methodology, in many cases encouraging reliance on a single methodological approach.

It is also possible, although fortunately less common, to hear of instances in which resource availability may have influenced research results. Two recent examples have received attention in the media. A genetics student painted a stripe down the backs of some of his rats. A panel of scientific experts, part of whose incomes came from the dairy industry, reported that cholesterol-rich foods, such as eggs and cream, would not increase the risk of heart trouble for normal, healthy adults. Such incidents are probably more likely to occur when interpretations are being made (for example, how much radioactivity is safe), rather than when evidence is being collected (as in the case of the genetics student).

As these examples indicate, amassing the necessary resources is an essential step in the research process. The inclusion of resource considerations in the garbage can model has two types of positive effects. First, it permits examination of the ways in which resource considerations can determine which theoretical problem is studied, which methodology is selected, and, possibly, even how the results of the research come out. Second, the inclusion of resources points out possible blind spots in the state of knowledge in a field; certain theoretical problems, methodologies, and solutions may be avoided due to resource considerations. Each of these types of blind spots is discussed below.

First, lack of resources may cause some theoretical problems to be ignored. For example, there has been considerable research concerning how blue-collar workers feel about comparisons made between their pay levels and those of other blue-collar workers (Blau, 1964; Homans, 1974; Patchen, 1961). There has been considerably less research concerning how blue-collar workers feel about the size of the labor/management pay differential (see Martin, 1981). One reason for this neglect is that organizations are reluctant to permit researchers to ask questions that might "stir up trouble." As this example indicates, difficulty of obtaining necessary resources, in this case access to a subject population, can determine what types of theoretical problems are addressed. This has the important effect of making it difficult to obtain resources for projects that challenge the political, economic, or intellectual status quo.

A second blind spot, pointed out by including resources in this model, is that some methodologies may not be used to address certain types of theoretical problems because of difficulty in obtaining resources. For example, a proposal involving the testing of a psychological hypothesis using large-scale survey methodology was submitted to a government funding agency. The proposal was returned, with the notation that the reviewers were dismayed that a standard-size budget had been requested, given that only one study was to be conducted. The psychological reviewers had obviously expected a proposal for a series of experiments, where the cost of each experiment would be less than the cost of a single large-scale survey. Although this particular proposal did eventually receive funding, difficulty of obtaining resources can mean that some types of theoretical problems seldom get addressed using some types of methodology.

Similar blind spots can occur when a lack of resources prohibits the "discovery" of certain solutions. If it can be anticipated that a given program of research will produce an undesirable type of outcome, funding can be denied. Such a resource allocation decision might be legitimate, as when the impact of a study on participants might be harmful. Such a decision can also be illegitimate. For example, a review panel can refuse to fund studies that challenge the findings of its own previous research or that put the institution it represents in a bad light. As these blind spots indicate, if access to needed resources is denied, some problems will never be addressed.

Consideration of the effects of the availability of resources has pointed out "sins of omission," such as the blind spots discussed above, and "sins of commission," whereby practical resource considerations influence the selection of theoretical problems, methods, and possibly even results. The omission or minimization of the role of resources in the rational model does not encourage examination of the myriad ways that resource considerations influence the research process and, therefore, the state of knowledge in a field.

Myth #2: The Nature of the Theoretical Problem Should Determine the Choice of Methodology. According to this second myth, the researcher begins by choosing a theoretical problem, and then matches the demands of that problem to the capabilities of a given methodology. In fact, methods are often selected for reasons that have little to do with theoretical considerations. Some of these reasons have been discussed above, as when resource availability determines the choice of a theoretical problem. It is also possible that a method may be available and be put to use without theoretical considerations. Thus, the SRC's Detroit Area Study might be characterized as a method in search of a theory. It is clear that, because of resource availability, survey methodology and sophisticated sampling techniques will be used. The theoretical focus of the questionnaire items is an open issue.

Just as a theoretical problem may float around looking for a theory to test, so a theoretical problem may rest in limbo until it comes into contact with a methodology capable of addressing it. This aspect of the garbage can model suggests another blind spot. Some theoretical problems are seldom addressed because of methodological difficulties. For example, a number of theories of human interaction have a "round robin" form. For example, what person A does may influence what person B does, which in turn influences what person A does. Such a round robin form is found in some theories of group dynamics (e.g., Bennis and Shepherd, 1970), dyadic communication, and the "enactment" of organizational reality (Weick, 1979). Many of these theoretical problems have generated relatively little empirical research, because the methodology necessary is difficult (e.g., Warner et al., 1979) or as yet unavailable.

Thus, methodological considerations often determine which theoretical problems are addressed. Both this second myth, and the myth described below, underestimate the causal impact of methodological considerations.

Myth #3: If Research Is Conducted Appropriately, Any Methodological Choice Should Lead to the Same Set of Theoretical Conclusions. The third myth is obviously overly optimistic, as indicated by Campbell and Fiske's (1959) discussion of methods variance. Although lip service is paid to the notion of methods variance, in fact, researchers often ignore this notion when they interpret the results of research that has relied on a single methodological approach. Thus, researchers often underestimate the extent to which their methodological choices influence which variables in a theoretical model are measured, which variables are relegated to the unmeasured "black box," and/or which theoretical conclusions are drawn from the data.

The classic solution to the methods variance problem is triangulation, according to the rational model. In actual practice, triangulation is seldom used. There are two types of reasons for this neglect: methodological and practical. The methodological reason is that the "technology of triangulation" is difficult and few consensual solutions to these difficulties are available.

The practical reasons for the avoidance of triangulation are often obvious. It is extremely costly. It takes more time, skills, and resources to design and execute two or three methodologically different studies (see Jick, 1979). Finally, use of multiple methods often does result in considerable methods variance and little convergent validity. This costly, often unpalatable, outcome need not be confronted if researchers confine themselves to a single methodology.

In addition, the advantages of triangulation, extolled in the textbooks, seldom surface in journal publications. Most journals tend to publish articles that rely on a restricted set of methodological choices. Reviewers sometimes suggest that the data collected with the less preferred methods be summarized in a short paragraph or relegated to a footnote. Consequently, any one journal article is likely to emphasize only one of the methods used, thus minimizing discussion of what was learned from triangulation.

For reasons such as these, triangulation is not often given the opportunity to prevent problems caused by methods variance. Instead, a single methodology is often relied upon. This permits a methodological choice to influence the nature of the theoretical outcomes of the research process.

Copy Myths —

Myth #4: Results Are the Endpoint, Not the Starting Point, of the Research Process. According to the rational model, the final step in the research process is a feedback loop, whereby the empirical results of a study are interpreted in light of the theoretical problem they were designed to address. In the garbage can model, the empirical results and their theoretical interpretations are labeled a "solution." The garbage can model makes no sequential assumptions about the relationship between that solution and the other variables in the model. Rather than the solution necessarily functioning as the endpoint of the research process, the garbage can model permits the solution to function as a starting point. This opens a number of possibilities.

The first of these possibilities is that the feedback loop is broken, so that the researcher makes no return to the theoretical problem that originally prompted the study. There are at least two ways this could happen. The theory could be irrelevant to the results found. Or, the results could not confirm the theory, in which case they could be ignored or a new theory devised to explain them.

Neither of these alternatives is necessarily an indication of low-quality research. Indeed, Skinner (1956) serendipitously discovered the first principles of behaviorism as an unanticipated outcome of a research project that had only a vague initial theoretical focus. Feyerabend (1975: 27) stresses the positive aspects of this approach, as "unreasonable, nonsensical foreplay which is necessary as a precondition for clarity and empirical success."

The second of these alternatives is less obviously benign. When results fail to confirm a theory, an ad hoc theoretical explanation of those results is often generated. The researcher has taken a set of results and has gone in search of a theory: "Have data, will travel." Such ad hoc explanations can be very useful. They can help us deal temporarily with the evolving failings of an old theory or with the initial start-up difficulties of a new theory (Feyerabend, 1975: 93). Whether one approves or disapproves of these two approaches taken, it is clear that both types of research violate the feedback loop stipulation of the rational model of the research process. Initial theories may be unrelated to at least some of the empirical results.

In addition to permitting violation of the feedback loop, the garbage can model also does not assume that the content of the solution is unknown until the end of the research. Relaxation of this assumption permits the solution to influence the availability of resources. Thus, research on some topics would not be funded by some sources unless the direction of the outcome were known or predictable with some certainty. For example, drug companies might be unlikely to fund psychological research on the effectiveness of non-drug-related treatments for hyperactive children unless they had reason to believe that the non-drug-related treatments were likely to be unsuccessful.

Similarly, if the content of the solution is known before the research process is begun, or if the researcher has firm expectations concerning the outcome, this may affect the choice of methodology. Thus, a method may be chosen because it is most likely to yield the expected solution. Indeed, in an extreme form of this position, experimental methodology has been criticized as being simply a laboratory demonstration to prove a point, rather than a methodology that is used to test a hypothesis (Feyerabend, 1975).

The garbage can model relaxes the stipulation that results must be interpreted in light of the original formulation of the theoretical problem, and does not assume that the content of the solution is unknown until the end of the research process. These shifts permit a solution to serve as the starting point of the research process, so that a solution can be the primary determinant of the availability of resources and the choice of a methodology. These factors contribute to the accuracy with which the garbage can model describes the actual process of research.

ADVANTAGES OF THE GARBAGE CAN AS A DESCRIPTIVE MODEL

The discussion above centered on four myths, derived from the rational model. Counterexamples congruent with the garbage can model demonstrated that those myths do not accurately represent the process by which research is actually conducted. The garbage can model is more successful than the rational model in providing an accurate presentation of the research process because it differs from the rational model in four important ways.

First, it suspends the sequential requirements of the rational model. The sequence of the steps in the rational model can be scrambled and, in some cases, reversed. The garbage can model conceptualizes research decisions as the product of Brownian motion, whereby the four variables (theoretical problems, resources, methodological choices, and solutions) attach and unattach themselves.

The second difference between the two models is that the garbage can model includes resources. This inclusion permits these practical considerations to function as a prime determinant of the choice of theoretical problem, methodological approach, and even, possibly, the nature of the solution.

The garbage can model also makes salient the importance of methodological choices. Available methodological choices can seek theoretical problems to address. Methodological choices can also determine resource availability and the nature of the solution found.

The final difference between the two models is that the garbage can model pinpoints blind spots in a field. Such blind spots include theoretical problems that may be neglected, due to lack of available resources or lack of an appropriate methodology. Likewise, certain methodologies may seldom be utilized and certain solutions never found.

One reason why these differences between the rational and garbage can models exist was discussed in the introduction to this section of the chapter: The objectives of the two models are different. The rational model does not aim to describe how research actually is conducted. Instead, it attempts to provide a description of how research should be publicly presented, perhaps how it should ideally be conducted.

If the garbage can model accurately describes the process of making research decisions, it may also accurately describe the quality of those decisions. The original formulation of the garbage can model has been used to investigate the quality of decisions in organizational contexts. To the extent that the leap from the original organizational to the research context is justified, the results of this organizational research may have implications concerning the quality of research decisions.

PITFALLS OF THE GARBAGE CAN APPROACH TO MAKING RESEARCH DECISIONS

The results of field studies (March and Olsen, 1976) and a computer simulation (Cohen et al., 1972) examine the advantages and disadvantages of the garbage can approach to decision making in organizational settings. Highlights of this research are discussed below in terms of relevance to the research process.

The primary finding of this research concerns the manner in which decisions are made. Three alternatives were investigated: resolution, flight, and oversight. Resolution occurs when a choice resolves a problem, in accord with the rational model. In research terms, resolution occurs when a methodological choice produces a solution that resolves a theoretical problem. Oversight occurs when related problems are overlooked while a choice is being made because other issues are attracting attention. For example, deadline pressures on other research projects could cause a methodological choice to be made by default. Flight occurs when related problems become occupied with other issues, so that a choice can be made without reference to these problems. When oversight and flight occur, a choice is made but it does not resolve the problem.

This research indicates that, contrary to the rational model, decisions were frequently made by flight and oversight, rather than resolution. This could have negative consequences in that organizations would "seem to make decisions without apparently making progress in resolving the problems that appear to be related to the decisions" (Cohen et al., 1972: 9). There is a possible parallel to the state of knowledge in the fields of social science. Current research efforts address, and often fail to resolve, issues which were first raised decades ago (see Festinger, 1981; Hastorf and Isen, forthcoming).

The debilitating effects of placing extra demands on an organization were also investigated. Under these conditions, flight and oversight were used even more frequently as methods of making choices. In addition, the process of decision making deteriorated. That is, the time it took to solve a problem, the number of times a decision maker shifted from one dilemma to another, and the difficulty of making a decision all increased. These results suggest that, when the demands on the research community increase, theoretical problems might be less likely to be solved, resources might be likely to shift from one problem to another more frequently, and methodological choices might be more likely to be time-consuming and less likely to resolve problems.

A final major finding of this research is that decision makers and problems tended "to move together from choice to choice. Thus, one would expect decision makers ... have a feeling they are always working on the same problems in somewhat different contexts, mostly without results" (Cohen et al., 1972: 10). This result implies that individual researchers, and other sources of resources such as funding agencies, might share a feeling of futility. Repeated efforts using different methodological approaches would fail to resolve a given problem. Problems addressed at an earlier time would return—still unresolved—to the same researcher or source of resources that previously proved unsuccessful. If this is an accurate description of the research process, it suggests that some late career scientists would sense a lack of real intellectual progress, and would, as a result, feel discouraged and/or bored.

LIMITATIONS AND IMPLICATIONS

The most important shortcomings of the garbage can model of the research process arise because it was designed to describe the process of making organizational, not research, decisions. The above discussion of research results is useful only insofar as the leap from the original organizational context to the research process is justified. Reasons for making this leap have been offered, but it remains a leap nevertheless.

The garbage can model has numerous other limitations. Perhaps the most notable concerns the variables that are not included in the model. These limitations are present even if the conceptualization of the model is expanded to include numerous garbage cans circulating in a larger space. For example, environmental forces such as historical trends, a paradigmatic revolution, or a political ideology could have dramatic impacts on the process of making research decisions. Such forces could set off a domino reaction. In the language of the model, given a push from a force in the environment, some garbage cans could set others tumbling; still other garbage cans could disappear from the field of action. The model, as currently constituted, has no way of incorporating systematically the effects of the environmental forces that are the province of sociology of knowledge and the philosophy and history of science. Although any model has variables it does not consider, this aspect of the model could clearly be strengthened.

Providing that the conceptual leap from the organizational to the research context is justified, the garbage can model can be both descriptively and prescriptively useful. As a descriptive model, it presents a metaphor for a research process in which some topics are seldom addressed, some theoretical problems are associated with a single methodological approach, some researchers find themselves addressing the same issues throughout their careers, some methods are rarely used, and sometimes the field appears to be making little progress.

If strong evidence of the relevance of the model to the research process were available, the model might have prescriptive implications. For example, students could be taught the model, and it might help them learn research "street smarts" or rules of thumb in a systematic rather than a haphazard fashion. In addition, the garbage can and rational models of the research process could be contrasted in order to pinpoint frequently occurring departures from the rational approach. The beneficial and detrimental aspects of those departures could then ‘be debated. Such training could give students a more accurate conception of the gap between rhetoric and reality, between how research decisions are made and how they ought to be made.

It is important to note the restricted nature of these prescriptions. They do not attack directly many of the potential pitfalls of the garbage can approach to making research decisions. There may be no realistic way to avoid some of the consequences of the garbage can approach to making research decisions without doing extreme violence to the principles of academic freedom. That game would not be worth that candle.

REFERENCES

ALLISON, G. T. (1969) "Conceptual models and the Cuban missle crisis." American Political Science Review 63: 689-718.

BENNIS, W. G. and H. A. SHEPHERD (1970) "A theory of group development," in T. M. Mills and S. Rosenberg (eds.) Readings in the Sociology of Small Groups. Englewood Cliffs, NJ: Prentice-Hall.

BERGER, P. L. and T. LUCKMANN (1966) The Social Construction of Reality. Garden City, NY: Doubleday.

BLAU, P. (1964) Exchange and Power in Social Life. New York: John Wiley.

CAMPBELL, D. T. and T. D. COOK (1979) Quasi-experimentation: Design and Analysis for Field Settings. Skokie, IL: Rand McNally.

——— and D. W. FISKE (1959) "Convergent and discriminant validation by the multitrait—multimethod matrix." Psychological Bulletin 56: 81-105.

COHEN, D., J. G. MARCH, and J. P. OLSEN (1972) "A garbage can model of organizational choice." Administrative Science Quarterly 17: 1-25.

CRANO, W. and M. BREWER (1973) Principles of Research in Social Psychology. New York: McGraw-Hill.

ELLSWORTH, P. C. (1977) "From abstract ideas to concrete instances: some guidelines for choosing natural research settings." American Psychologist 32: 604-615.

FESTINGER, L. (1981) Four Decades of Social Psychology. London: Oxford University Press.

FEYERABEND, P. (1975) Against Method. London: NLB, Humanities Press.

HASTORF, A. and A. ISEN (forthcoming) Cognitive Social Psychology. New York: Elsevier North-Holland.

HOMANS, G. (1974) Social Behavior: Its Elementary Forms. New York: Harcourt Brace Jovanovich.

JICK, T. D. (1979) "Mixing qualitative and quantitative methods: triangulation in action." Administrative Science Quarterly 24: 602-611.

KUHN, T. S. (1970) Structure of Scientific Revolutions. Chicago: University of Chicago Press.

LINDBLOM, C. E. (1965) The Intelligence of Democracy. New York: Macmillan.

MARCH, J. G. and J. P. OLSEN (1976) Ambiguity and Choice in Organizations. Bergen, Norway: Universitels Forlaget.

MARCH, J. G. and H. A. SIMON (1958) Organizations. New York: John Wiley.

MARTIN, J. (1981) "Relative deprivation: a theory of distributive injustice for an era of shrinking resources," in L. Cummings and B. Staw (eds.) Research in Organizational Behavior (Vol. 3). Greenwich, CT: JAI Press.

PATCHEN, M. (1961) The choice of wage comparisons. Englewood Cliffs, NJ: Prentice-Hall.

RUNKEL, P. J. and J. E. McGRATH (1972) Research on Human Behavior: A Systematic Guide to Method. New York: Holt, Rinehart & Winston.
SELLTIZ, C., M. JAHODA, M. DEUTSCH, and S. W. COOK (1959) Research Methods in Social Relations. New York: Holt, Rinehart & Winston.
SKINNER, B. F. (1956) "A case history in scientific method." American Psychologist 11: 221-233.
STARK, W. (1967) The Sociology of Knowledge. London: Routledge & Kegan Paul.
WARNER, R. M., D. A. KENNY, and M. SOTO (1979) "A new round robin analysis of variance for social interaction data." Journal of Personality and Social Psychology 37: 1741-1757.
WEBB, E. J. and P. C. ELLSWORTH (1975) "On nature and knowing," in H. W. Sinaiko and L. A. Broedling (eds.) Perspectives on Attitude Measurement: Surveys and Their Alternatives. Washington, DC: Smithsonian Institution.
WEBB, E. J., D. T. CAMPBELL, R. D. SCHWARTZ, and L. SECHREST (1972) Unobtrusive Measures: Non Reactive Research in the Social Sciences. Skokie, IL: Rand McNally.
WEICK, K. (1979) The Social Psychology of Organizing. Reading, MA: Addison-Wesley.

2

Idiosyncrasy and Circumstance

Choices and Constraints in the Research Process

Richard A. Kulka

□ As in the investigation of any other significant behavioral research phenomenon, one who seeks to study or describe factors related to the research process itself is under some obligation to identify and document the present "state of the art" on this topic, including not only the state of scholarship but also the state of practice in this area. In contemplating this duty with regard to the study of decisions, or "judgment calls," in the social research process, this task is especially formidable, since written documentation of research practice on this topic is widely and thinly scattered throughout the literature and probably somewhat biased. There is substantial variation in the value placed on such writing by researchers themselves, as well as by the organizations and disciplines with which they happen to be affiliated. In addition, much of value in this area has likely not as yet appeared in print, thereby

Author's Note: The concept underlying this article and its execution emerged in discussion with Joseph McGrath, Joanne Martin, and Barry Staw, to whom I am grateful for their helpful advice and comments. In addition, a special note of appreciation and gratitude is due to Lawrence Cummings, John R.P. French, Jr., Gerald

requiring that one find a way of supplementing the written word in order to adequately document the state of the art.

How then does one describe the state of the art in this area? Paradigmatic descriptions of the conduct of research, such as the "garbage can model of the research process" recently elaborated by Joanne Martin (1981) offer a partial answer to this question, in that they seek to provide a more realistic description of the process by which social research is *actually* conducted than that implied by the conventional "rational" model of the research process. As such, these models establish a foundation for developing a "descriptive" rather than a "normative" methodology in social research (see Bell and Newby, 1977). They might be regarded as yet another instance of what Babbie (1979: 22) dubs "the iconoclastic view of science," if it were not for the fact that, as Martin and others (Bell and Newby, 1977; Horowitz, 1969; Platt, 1976) have noted, virtually everyone who has done any research is *already aware* of the considerable divergence between how research is actually done and what is found in professional journals and conventional methodological textbooks. Thus, for example, I believe that most organizational researchers would hardly find surprising the following characterization of methodological decision making offered by Daniel Katz (1980) in a recent interview:

> Researchers are not free and open to consider all possibilities. They are under constraints of various sorts and these con-

---

Gurin, Richard Hackman, Rosabeth Kanter, Daniel Katz, Arnold Tannenbaum, Joseph Veroff, the late Philip Brickman, and the late Angus Campbell, all of whom generously granted time to be interviewed in connection with this project and subsequently provided eloquent and candid accounts of critical decisions in their own research, chronicles upon which much of this article is based. It is important to note, however, that the quotations cited by these eminent scholars were provided in the context of an explicit request to reflect on choices and constraints in the research process and should not be construed as representative of their general philosophies or evaluations of social science research. In each case, they agreed to provide these examples of research decisions in the hope that such descriptions will serve to enlighten and strengthen future research efforts.

straints become very important in the decisions that get made. In other words, there is much less rational decision-making than one would expect from a course in which you outline how you set up a research design, how you implement the research design, and how you execute it. What happens in reality is much more at a pragmatic level. People do what they can do in given situations. Often they don't have enough vision. Often they make too many compromises, but compromises have to be made. The real essential point is not to compromise too much.

It is a series of restraints the whole way. You have the restraint, of course, in the way of resources. Most researchers have had more projects turned down and not been funded than they have had projects funded. Resources are only available for certain types of things. . . . It's also in the interest of the *zeitgeist* of the time as to what will get funded and what won't get funded . . . there are constraints of facilities. There aren't the facilities to carry on research in an open way in the social field. There are the constraints of time. . . . People are expected to come up with reports and with journal articles and books, and this puts them under time pressures. To lay out a program of research where you first develop all your measures and then go ahead and use them is ideal, but difficult to achieve practically. There are the constraints of being part of the social situation, in that there are things you can't observe, you aren't permitted to observe. There are questions you are not permitted to ask. . . . This doesn't cover all the constraints, but these are some of them.

Hence, although one is tempted to assume that "the rationality of the final (research) product is a consequence of the rationality of the method for realizing that product" (Horowitz, 1969: 9), most practicing researchers are well aware that there is a pervasive subjective side to research methodology and that "there are practical social contingencies in doing empirical research that have consequences for its progress and outcome" (Platt, 1976: 9). In short, there is widespread recognition that "idiosyncrasies of person and circumstance are at the heart not the periphery of the scientific enterprise" (Johnson, cited in Bell and Newby, 1977: 9).

But where do researchers get such knowledge? Partly from reading methodological appendices and other written documents, perhaps, but in large part from conversations with others about research—from the gossip, anecdotes, and folklore that pervade research units—and from their own research experience. Seldom indeed does a published piece of research devote much attention to the human problems involved in formulating a researchable problem and executing the project. One searches largely in vain in our professional journals for an account of dead ends entered, fortuitous coincidences discovered, or striking encounters with other problems, which we all know are an integral part of translating a clever idea into a piece of research as conventionally reported in the professional journals (see Wilson, 1978). Moreover, "because most research-methods texts, like research monographs, deal exclusively with the context of justification, matters related to the context of discovery are seldom found in print" (Hammond, 1964: 3).

In sum, traditional research methods textbooks generally deal only with a few of the problems one encounters, and research papers and monographs rarely record the many choices, decisions, and refinements made along the way. Methodological preferences are seldom made clear, the implications of personal and pragmatic considerations and constraints, which may influence one's choices and restrict one's possibilities, are frequently ignored, and the many compromises and modifications that are made as a result of circumstances are generally omitted from the final product (Golden, 1976).

In essence, although most research reports in the social sciences contain a fairly extensive description of methods chosen, few indeed provide a very informative account of the processes by which these choices came about. In an effort to fill that gap—to better communicate the *sub rosa* phases of contemporary social research to the apprentice researcher—a number of books have appeared in recent years that provide rich and candid chronicles of the process of social research by eminent and experienced researchers, as well as by relative novices (e.g., Golden, 1976). These have appeared under such titles as: *Sociologists at Work* (Hammond, 1964), *Political Scientists at Work* (Walter, 1971), *Doing Sociological Research* (Bell and Newby, 1977), *Social and Educational Research in Action* (Wilson, 1978), *Realities of Social Research* (Platt, 1976), and *The Research Experience* (Golden, 1976).

As a result of these efforts, detailed and candid descriptions of the process by which significant methodological decisions actually get made are in much greater abundance now than they were ten to fifteen years ago. Yet, considerably more such material needs to be generated if we are to better understand the state of the art with regard to methodological choice in behavioral and social science. The principal reason we need to do so is that, to date, there is little evidence to suggest that the lessons to be learned from these previous accounts have been well assimilated into the research enterprise. But what are these lessons, and of what value can they be? Consider first an observation by Laurie Broedling (1975: 4) in her introduction to *Perspective on Attitude Assessment: Surveys and Their Alternatives:*

> It is apparent from this description that if all necessary issues were seriously considered, decisions regarding methods would never get made because they would be impossibly complicated. Yet such decisions are made every day—which attests to the fact that the way in which methods actually get chosen does not conform to the ideal process. If the existing methodological selection process is to be improved, however, it is essential to describe and explain that process. In other words, increasing methodological self-awareness is a necessary prerequisite to deciding what improvements can and should be made.

In effect, the systematic accumulation and evaluation of candid, extensive, and realistic descriptions of the process of doing behavioral and social science research may result in an "informal methodological guidebook" (Horowitz, 1969) of sorts, a supplement to conventional methods textbooks that suggests more realistic prescriptions for the conduct of successful research (see Platt, 1976).

The rest of this chapter contains a number of examples of such choices and constraints in the social research process that may serve to illustrate the state of the art with regard to how methodological decisions are actually made in behavioral and social science research. Some are examples taken from "candid asides" or "embarrassed footnotes" in articles published in the professional journals, but they are few indeed. From a review of the articles appearing in each of four journals over three to five years, it appears that less than one article in forty contains such a description. Other examples to be presented are excerpts from a series of informal interviews with eminent researchers on some of the methodological decisions they have made in the course of their own research. Finally, some of the examples are research anecdotes taken from some of the already published chronicles noted earlier. This chapter is organized to deal with logical decisions at each of three major stages of the research process: (a) formulating the research problem, (b) designing the study, including the selection of settings, strategies, and subjects, and (c) executing the design, including measurement and operationalization of variables and data collection.

FORMULATING THE RESEARCH PROBLEM

It is rare for a social scientist to report the very early stages of a major research project, to devote much attention to the actual reasons why he or she undertook the project (Leege and Francis, 1974; Wilson, 1978). One noted scholar, when asked to describe how he became interested in a given topic, mused that a question posed in that manner will generally yield the same type of response that an interviewer is likely to get by asking a politician how he or she became interested in politics. Both questions "run the risk of equally windy, self-serving, and unrevealing replies" (Matthews, 1971: 9-10). Nevertheless, a number of eminent researchers have provided realistic and revealing accounts of their original reasons for undertaking significant pieces of social research.

Perhaps the classic accounts in this area are those that relate the way in which resource availability, such as government funding or organizational competence, may influence the choice of a theoretical problem, a feature of the research process noted by Martin as standing in stark contrast to the assumption that resources are important only as enabling conditions. For example, it is not unusual for a major research organization to undertake a study primarily because a particular foundation or other funding source decides to allocate a considerable amount of money to a given issue at some point in time. Organizational constraints on problem choice may, of course, also take a number of other forms, as illustrated in this segment from an interview with an academic researcher in England conducted by Platt (1976: 115):

> "I was an untenured member of staff, needing to do some research relevant to the needs of the department. . . . I'd been asked to do several other things in this department and refused."
>
> "Did you not think of doing some research of your own?"
>
> "No, the research of my own was being done primarily about (other field), but this was regarded by the department as nothing to do with their interests . . . it was necessary to be seen doing something relevant to the department's interest."

Implicit here is recognition of the fact that our current academic reward system often plays a powerful role in decisions about what to study, a factor that is made even more explicit by Richard Hackman (1980) in an interview about his research on groups:

> I almost couldn't have afforded to pursue it otherwise because the reward system in which I was operating did require me to be productive. If you take out of my resume everything but the group stuff, it's pretty thin. There is not that much group stuff, even though it extends all the way back to the beginning. It is exceedingly hard, exceeding expensive to do a group study. You can run 22 cognitive psych studies or 22 attitude change studies in the period of time it takes you to do one good group study. I don't think I could have made a career—I couldn't have had a successful career—if I had stayed exclusively in groups.

Institutional constraints on problem choice may also be *positive*, of course, as noted by the late Philip Brickman:

> One of the constraints I think that we don't recognize quite so well is the constraint placed upon us by our successes, and what other people in turn think of us and think about us, expect from us, et cetera. . . . I think something that constrains a lot of people's research in ways that they don't fully realize is that they do a variety of things and get a response for some of them, become the experts at something, and thereafter receive invitations to do things—contribute to other books and conferences, et cetera—because they have already done those things. So the field tends to push us to sing the songs that have been the hits.

Other factors influencing the decision of what to study tend to reflect idiosyncrasies of the person rather than of the organization, including aspects of personal history or preference, as emphasized by Hackman:

> This is going to sound kind of sappy. I really do want to understand groups. There is something in me that makes me want to understand it. . . . I think, as bizarre as this may sound . . . as a child I may have actually been in a group and that may have just set this off. I think it's rooted in me pretty deep whatever it is. There is something in me that says, "Hackman,

keep going on it because you are going to understand these things," and it's become my "great white whale."

Or, the personal element may be a subjective reaction to a given state of affairs in the political or research enterprise, as in the case of Rosabeth Kanter's (1980) decision to pursue research on men and women in organizations (e.g., Kanter, 1977; Kanter and Stein, 1979):

> I did not enter this field the way some researchers do, which is to see a new field like the study of women as a chance for me to carve out a niche. I did it out of *annoyance*. I felt that research that was narrowly psychological, that looked at people outside of any context whatsoever, and then made generalizations (without) taking into account the setting which was pushing them to do those things, was very misleading, to say the least. And so, what was coming out, mostly in the psychological but also in the sociological literature, were a number of statements about how different women were. Well, I was a woman in organizations, and I know that those generalizations did not apply to me. Yet I could see the pressures in my own situation, and that of others, that might lie behind the stereotypes.
>
> Similarly, because I was doing the study of commitment in the sales force, I was interacting with a number of men in sales. . . . So I observed that there were some men who behaved the way women did, and vice versa. For many of the women I was meeting, the stereotyped "research findings" simply didn't fit. And so, I was very annoyed that these generalizations were being flung around and were being used to stereotype women in a new way, inappropriately, with perhaps negative political consequences and without much guidance for organizational change. I had a personal need to demystify a lot of stereotypes, and to show the way settings push people into certain characteristic behaviors.

DESIGNING THE STUDY

Decisions in the design stage involve the choice of setting, research strategy, and sample or subjects. Although we are all aware that in practice these design considerations overlap a great deal, let us consider each separately in turn.

RESEARCH SETTINGS

When one considers the question of selecting a research site or setting, the question of _access_ is the principal constraint that readily comes to mind. Most behavioral and social science researchers would likely agree that accessibility is frequently the predominant criterion in selecting a setting in which to do one's research. A classic description of this problem is Peter Blau's (1964) chronicle of how he happened to choose two government agencies in which to study *The Dynamics of Bureaucracy* (Blau, 1955: 20-21):

> On the suggestion of (Robert) Merton, from whose criticism and advice I benefited greatly at this stage, I modified my plan and decided to compare groups in two bureaucracies—a public and a private one. I reformulated my hypotheses in terms of this comparison between government agency and large private firm and spent much of the summer trying to obtain permission for study from one organization of each type. The immediate cause for abandoning this plan was that I was unable to obtain permission for doing this research from any suitable private firm, but by the time I had to make this decision there were other reasons for it, too. My experience with the first agency made me realize that, since I had so much more to learn about social patterns in government agencies, a comparison of groups in two government agencies which differ in some ways but are not too dissimilar might be most fruitful.

Given the substantial impact of Blau's study on subsequent research and theory in organizational research, one cannot help but wonder what would have happened if he *had* been granted access to a private firm!

As we all know, however, initial access to an organizational setting does not assure *continued* access, a vulnerability that is highlighted in a dramatic way in the description of a recent study of "environmental intervention for litter control" reported by Scott Geller and his colleagues (1977: 348):

> Changing grocery stores had not been planned; the littering procedure implemented in the present study provoked a managerial order that we leave Radford Brothers.

On a more serious note, the vulnerability of one's choice of research settings to unforeseen events outside one's control, in spite of meticulous efforts to anticipate all contingencies, is poignantly illustrated in Arnold Tannenbaum's (1980) account of his international study of organizational hierarchies (Tannenbaum et al., 1974):

> The decision was made to include a number of specific countries, and agreement was reached collaboratively between me and colleagues in the respective countries that we would go forward together.

> Two of the countries that agreed—that is, colleagues from those countries agreed—were Yugoslavia and Israel. Yugoslavia has the so-called workers' self-management system, and therefore we saw the possibility of studying these Marxian-inspired organizations. In Israel we had organizations from the Kibbutzim, which also are based on Marxian ideological principles. Shortly after we got the grant, however, the Six-Day War broke out, and Yugoslavia broke relations with Israel. My Yugoslav colleague said that he couldn't participate in the project. Boy, was that a problem.

> I think it illustrates the saliency of politics of ideology to ventures of this kind, international collaborative ventures. Politics . . . inevitably enters, but often in more subtle and sublimated ways. This was especially problematic, especially serious, since, as I said before, we had a small pool only of organizations of this type, and, if Yugoslavia dropped out, half of our pool disappeared. . . . We managed to get out of trouble fortunately by locating another colleague in Yugoslavia who was willing to join the project.

This example, of course, represents a particularly dramatic case of the influence of external factors on the choice of research settings. Realistically, the choice of setting(s) in most organizational research likely reflects a considerably more mundane set of factors, such as those described by McKelvey and Kilmann (1975: 28) in their article on organization design:

The organization studied was the management school of a large university. It was chosen because its dean and faculty members wanted to change its structure, not because it was especially representative of all management schools; nevertheless, it was not unlike other management schools and departments the authors were familiar with, except that it was larger than most, having 115 faculty members.

And, although the conventional reason given for the use of classroom settings for social research is convenience and ease of access, the late Philip Brickman provided a somewhat different slant on this choice:

One thing that I have done sometimes is a kind of compromise in choice of setting between a laboratory, where you are picking up something that's of limited duration and limited stakes, to a real life setting. . . . I have used classes. Classes have the advantage of involving students in a role in a setting where it's part of their lives. They are working hard and they really care about it, and it runs for months. And yet, if you are the teacher, you don't have to negotiate enormously difficult problems of access. It is much easier to do research. In fact, it's barely possible to do research unless you have some power in the situation and people feel that they have something to gain by helping you to do the research. It may simply be your admiration and respect. It may be the value that they attach to participating in the progress of science. It may be money; it may be credit; it may be a lot of different things.

Parenthetically, the implicit or explicit role of power and exchange in other research decisions has also been cogently described by Herbert Kelman (1972) and others (McCarthy and McCarthy, 1975).

RESEARCH STRATEGIES

The choice of a particular research strategy is a decision that exerts a powerful effect on virtually all other aspects of the research. Choice of a research strategy can and often does reflect a fairly rational decision process, not unlike that suggested by the ideal model of the research process that is so often disparaged. For example, consider the process described by Daft and Bradshaw (1980: 442-443):

> Answers about new departments might be obtained from three sources: organizational records, observation of events leading to development of new departments, or interviews and question-naires. Organizational records (mostly minutes of faculty senate meetings) contained only official information and did not provide enough information. Observations could not be used because observers would have had to be present before the new department was formed, sometimes a period of several years. Thus the best record of relevant events and processes was the memories of people who participated in the formation of the new departments. This source could be tapped through personal interviews with selected informants.

Let us not delude ourselves, however, into believing that the pieces always fall so neatly into place this way. Indeed, the most common assertion made with regard to method choice in this area is that researchers largely choose the research strategies they are most familiar with, giving little consideration to alternative strategies that might be applied to a given research problem. Kaplan (1964: 28) calls this the "law of the instrument," a principle analogous to the well-known "law of the hammer" ("Give a small boy a hammer, and he will find that everything needs pounding!"). Martin Trow (1957: 35), however, suggests a somewhat different analogy:

> Every cobbler thinks leather is the only thing. Most social scientists, including the present writer, have their favorite methods with which they are familiar and have some skill in using. And I suspect we mostly choose to investigate problems that seem vulnerable to attack through these methods. But we should at least try to be less parochial than cobblers. Let us be done with the arguments of "participant observation" *versus* interviewing—as we have largely dispensed with the arguments for psychology *versus* sociology—and get on with the business of attacking our problems with the widest array of conceptual and methodological tools that we possess and they demand.

Although most researchers are somewhat reluctant to own up to being a bit parochial in this regard, consider a candid admission by Herbert Gans (1962: 336) in his description of methods used in his study of the *Urban Villagers*:

> Having been trained in sociology at the University of Chicago during the era when Everett C. Hughes and the late Louis Wirth—to name only two—were dominant influences in the Department of Sociology, I believed strongly in the value of participant-observation as a method of social research. As a result, I felt that I could best achieve my study purposes by living in a slum myself.

More often, however, instances of the role of personal preferences and other constraints on the choice of a research strategy take a more subtle form. Consider first a description by Charles Wright (Wright and Hyman, 1964) of why he and Herbert Hyman chose *not* to use participant observation in their evaluation study (Hyman et al., 1962: 127):

> At one point in our planning, we considered the collection of data through participant observation, but we decided against this for several reasons. First, the limitations imposed by the

available funds prohibited hiring a full-time observer. Consequently one of us—probably I—would have had to assume that
role. We feared that a full-time immersion into the Encampment culture would have cut seriously into my time available
for such other essential research tasks as the design of questionnaires and would also have entailed the risk of reducing my
objectivity as an evaluator as I, perhaps, became socialized by
the program. Second, we feared that constant observation of
the campers during forty-two days of the program would make
the research too obtrusive and interfere with the natural atmos-
phere of the Encampment, thereby even spoiling the major
evaluation itself.

Earlier in this same chronicle, Wright noted that one of the
primary reasons he found the Encampment's problem tempt-
ing was that it provided an opportunity to apply some novel
evaluation research methods.

A final example, taken from a research chronicle by Robert
Moore (1977) describing his decision to use a survey in a study
of *Race, Community and Conflict* (Rex and Moore, 1967: 99)
in Birmingham, England, illustrates the political or strategic
factors that influence the choice of a particular research
method, along with yet another variation on the influence of
resources on methodological choice:

> From the very beginning it was clear that a more formal survey
> of the locality was necessary. The data I was collecting were
> sociologically rich and socially colourful, and they could be
> used to make sense of what was happening in Sparkbrook. But
> my meetings with people were based on introductions from
> friends or relatives or were haphazard; I approached organisa-
> tions through their officers. How typical, in the statistical sense,
> were the people I had met? How widely held were the views I
> had heard expressed in cafes, pubs and churches? Did my face
> or my manner invite particular kinds of meetings or evoke
> particular opinions? I felt that a more "objective" survey would
> provide an important check on the rest of my work. At a more
> general level a survey was also important in terms of the public
> presentation of the research. It would be easier to reject our

findings if it was held that I had only spoken to selected people and that no attempt had been made to sample opinions generally in Sparkbrook. In addition, a little money was available for a survey, so it seemed sensible to conduct a questionnaire survey of a sample of the Sparkbrook population.

SUBJECTS, GROUP, OR SAMPLE

Ostensibly, other things being equal, the subjects or groups to be studied are usually determined by the nature of the research problem (or vice versa, if one relaxes these sequential assumptions of the "rational modal," as specified by the garbage can model suggested by Martin, 1981). Other things are rarely equal, however, and a number of subjective and pragmatic considerations impact on the choice of whom to study. Consider, for example, a set of criteria proposed by Joy Browne (1976: 72) for choosing a group to study:

> To my way of thinking, there are four reasons for choosing one group over another: the group should be fun, accessible, convenient, and suitable. Lest these criteria be dismissed as frivolous, let me explain. Fieldwork is exhausting, difficult, psychologically demanding, and time-consuming. The more fun and interesting the group, the greater the likelihood that your interest and commitment will be sustained. A fun group can be just as important as a dull group, and a lot easier to study.
>
> Accessibility is crucial. A group that is physically inaccessible is an obvious stumbling block, but an emotionally or psychologically inaccessible group is equally, if more subtly, an inappropriate choice. For example, a group of nuns I chose to study via participant observation was so psychologically inaccessible that I was counting ballpoint pen clicks for lack of more relevant data. It is impossible to learn very much about a group from a long distance, whether it be physical or psychological space.
>
> Convenience is the key to good research. The more often you can be on the scene, the more you will learn. And the more convenient the group is, the more often you can be on the scene.

Suitability is a time bomb with a long fuse. Often it is not until a study has progressed, or at least continued for some length of time, that it becomes obvious whether the group is suitable for study in terms of relevance to theory and method, personability of the researcher, and time constraints.

Note that these latter dimensions of suitability, personability, and time constraints have little to do with the nature of the problem.

Similarly, a number of studies, while giving careful consideration to both theoretical and methodological issues in defining the units to be studied, are forced to defer once again to the dictates of resource availability when all is said and done, as in a study reported by Kim Cameron (1978: 611):

Student representatives were not included in the study's dominant coalition because (1) students are not generally in a position to directly influence the direction and functioning of the institution; (2) they generally have more limited information about the overall institution than do other dominant coalition members; (3) they have been found in other studies not to differ significantly in their perceptions of the institution from faculty members or administrators; and most importantly; (4) constraints on time and money prohibited a representative sample from being gathered from relevant student groups on various campuses.

Yet another case in which practical limitations essentially define the specific groups to be studied is given by Cornelius and Lyness (1980: 157):

Four organizations in the Columbus, Ohio, metropolitan area participated in this study on a volunteer basis. Jobs included were cleanup and sanitation worker, laboratory technician, production supervisor, mechanic, production worker, bank encoder, bank key entry, bank teller, computer operator, and customer services representative. The major criterion used to select jobs for inclusion in the study was that at least nine incumbents performed the same basic tasks.

A final example of how both strategic and practical considerations may influence the particular group of people selected for a given study is reflected in both the mission and structure of most national survey organizations. In part, such organizations exist and persist because for many purposes national data are of greater interest and utility than state or local data. In turn, because such organizations are explicitly constituted and organized to conduct national surveys, it is typically easier for them to study the nation than a particular state, even the state or region in which they are located.

EXECUTING THE STUDY DESIGN

Having illustrated the crucial role that idiosyncrasy and circumstance play in research design, it should come as no surprise that personal and pragmatic considerations and constraints also exert a significant influence on the actual execution of social research, leaving their mark on both the measurement and operationalization of variables and on the data collection process itself.

OPERATIONALIZATION OF VARIABLES

Although the process by which theoretical constructs become operational measures is most often portrayed in the research literature as a matter subject to utmost rigor and rationality, one does not have to venture very far into the folklore to find that in practice measurement decisions generally represent an uneasy compromise among several conflicting desiderata, once again reflecting idiosyncrasies of both person and circumstance. Perhaps the most obvious empirical illustrations of the constraints of reality on one's choice of measures are evident in studies forced to rely on measures from *existing* data to represent a desired construct, as in Judith Blau and William McKinley's (1979: 206) study of the impact of ideas on successful organizational innovation:

> Various considerations indicated that the best measure of successful innovation is the number of architectural awards won by the firm during the past five years. The faculty response in evaluating firms was poor: only 120 of the approximately 300 returned questionnaires. The difficulty with using journal articles to measure organizational innovation is that they often credit a firm's top design architect without indicating whether the work described is that of the individual or the firm.

A more subtle influence on choice of measure, and one of potentially greater consequence, is suggested by Rosabeth Kanter (1980):

> Research is more personalized as people actually do it than ever is reflected when they report the results, and researchers often have to scramble to find a rationale for asking particular questions. So it is far easier to fall back on repeating what someone else did, as though that creates automatic legitimacy, as though a set of survey items someone else used is automatically better than newly created ones. The justifications are familiar in a lot of the literature, and probably account for why so much of it seems so trivial, like: "The following ten past researchers asked these questions, so I guess it's all right for me to ask them too." In other words, such researchers avoid personal responsibility, and I'm saying I *take* personal responsibility when I ask my own questions. That's how you learn something new.

Lest one fail to recognize the basic rationale behind such a choice (if not the specific motivation), consider a description of "research method" in a recent issue of the *Academy of Management Journal* in a report by Joseph Champoux (1980: 467):

> Data were obtained with either the short form or the long form of the Job Diagnostic Survey. . . . The Job Diagnostic Survey

(JDS) was selected for this research because it was used in the original study. . . . Furthermore, it was specifically developed from the job characteristics model of work motivation and has been used in all of the basic research done with this model. . . . The use of this instrument in the present study permits an extension of that line of research without introducing differences due to difference in measurement.

In citing this example, I do not mean to imply that the decision by Champoux to employ the widely used JDS was either incorrect or due to some ulterior motive. What is important to recognize, however, is that the choice here is, in Joseph McGrath's (1981) terms, "dilemmatic." One is forced to choose between two mutually incompatible goals, in this case between the extension of a promising line of research without introducing measurement differences and the opportunity potentially to add something quite new to the "body of knowledge" by using a different set of measures.

At times, of course, the decision to pursue a different line of questioning than that followed in previous research reflects a quite different set of motives. For example, an explicit and legitimate goal of much research is to influence policy decisions, and certain concepts and measurement strategies are obviously better suited for that purpose than others. Specifically, research employing concepts or measures that most closely approximate the terminology and concerns of legislators, government officials, and other decision makers is more likely to be effective in influencing policy decisions than that employing more diffuse concepts derived from typical academic research.

Finally, consider a series of three poignant examples that illustrate the broad range of factors that may influence the development of a typical research questionnaire. First, a candid confession by an English researcher interviewed by Jennifer Platt (1976: 21), suggesting an influence to which many are likely subject, but few willing to admit:

One was not sure what one wanted to explain, and because of this, and because the questionnaire contained a large number of open-ended questions, there was the immediate problem of how to code it . . . we took out as little as possible; we were going to assume the existence of large and powerful and also free computer facilities, and have to use those to construct higher-order codings. This decision was very much influenced by the fact that we had excellent computer facilities, and also the fact that I had become very interested in computers. . . . And so we adopted the strategy of coding which was fantastically diffuse and general, and an immense number of punched cards, so that for instance question 27 became 3 punched cards! . . . So then we put an enormous amount of labour into producing these descriptive tables, so we had an immense amount of descriptive bumf lying around. . . . It's not finished now, and it doesn't seem likely that it ever will be finished.

A more complex but equally candid decision process is provided by James Davis (1964) in his description of "questionnaire evolution" in his classic study of *Great Books and Small Groups* (Davis, 1961: 221-226):

When it comes to writing a questionnaire, the sky is the limit; or rather, one's guess as to how lengthy a document the respondents will complete without rebellion is the only boundary.

A certain amount of disagreement arose among the parties: the Fund for Adult Education backing two horses, the Great Books Foundation a third, and the study director a dark fourth horse. The first horse was "community participation," a matter of considerable interest to the Fund for Adult Education, which was convinced that participation in Great Books should and maybe even did lead people to become more active in community affairs.

The Great Books Foundation maintained . . . that . . . all . . . that participants were expected to become . . . (was) more sophisticated, more critical in their thinking, broader in their approach, and so on, whether or not they chose to favor the left, right, center, or to refrain from community life.

At this point, the inevitable answer occurred: to stress both purely intellectual and also community-participation materials. However . . . the compromise decision actually became a sellout of the Great Books Foundation's position.

What should have been a series of technical measures of cognitive functioning became a set of crude information measures along with considerable materials on aesthetics and ideologies. Part of the shift can be explained by . . . the inability of the Great Books Foundation to come up with neat objectives for which nice tests exist, but a good proportion came from the wily maneuvers of the study director.

This is the intellectual history of the questionnaire, a lengthy document bearing the stamp of the Fund for Adult Education's interest in community participation, some vestigial traces of the foundation's interest in "critical thinking," a lot of my own penchant for materials on aesthetics and ideologies, and a good bit of information on functional roles, inserted as a substitute for . . . excised sociometric items.

In a number of research projects, of course, the role of the client or sponsor is somewhat more encompassing than that suggested by Davis, as illustrated in Jennifer Platt's (1976: 56) summary of interviews conducted with a number of practicing researchers throughout the United Kingdom:

Whether or not assumptions differed, clients often affected the way in which the research was done. The choice of sample was affected in several cases by the sponsor's insistence on the inclusion or exclusion of certain groups. Sometimes this did not make much substantive difference, except to the expense of the project: a semi-governmental body insisted that Scotland be included, although there were few instances there of the kind to be studied, and another wanted wives of a group of employees being studied to be interviewed too. In other instances the effect was more serious: it was insisted that a whole population be approached rather than a sample, or that comparative samples relevant to assessing the impact of a measure be not included. The questions asked in surveys could also be influenced: a private organisation asked for the inclusion of a lot of detailed questions in one area, the main effect of which was a large increase in the bulk of data to be analysed without a corresponding increase in the interest of the results; in a project commissioned by a governmental body questions on politics and religion were not allowed to be included.

THE DATA COLLECTION PROCESS

A final set of research anecdotes relates to decisions made during the data collection process itself, a period generally fraught with many compromises and modifications made in the face of changing circumstances. Such decisions are often left out of the final research product, although there are a number of examples of such detours and compromises in the research literature. Consider first a typical compromise described in a study by Dennis Dossett and his colleagues (1980: 563):

> Organizational constraints prevented the random assignment of equal proportions of respondents to the three anonymity/authority conditions. Supervisors were selected to participate in the experiment based on their availability and their representativeness of supervisory positions in the company.

Another typical operational problem frequently encountered in the course of data collection emerged in a study described by Martin Greller (1980: 25) in a recent report on the evaluation of feedback sources:

> Nineteen foremen completed the subordinate version of the questionnaire, whereas only 8 of the 19 completed the supervisor version. The foremen were unable to complete both forms when the questionnaires were administered first thing in the morning; they had to leave with their subordinates to begin the day's work. During administrations later in the day, foremen were able to complete both forms. This problem did not occur with first line managers, whose work schedules allowed them to complete both forms. Assignment to early morning sessions was a matter of administrative convenience and was not related to supervisor or work group characteristics.

Naturally, some more dramatic examples of how a research project can be modified considerably over the course of data collection are also available. One especially candid illustration is provided by David Reisman and Jeanne Watson (1964: 258-259) in their description of the evolution of a data collection strategy for their study of "sociability":

> Thus, all of [us] found that the basic assumption underlying the research proposal was untenable: we could not recruit individual subjects to respond *both* to interviews and tests *and* to observation.

> A logical next step was to try to recruit subjects for purposes of observation only. . . . [One] version of this technique was to stage a party for persons whom one knew only peripherally. . . . In every case [where we tried], the attempt to convert a peripheral relationship into one permitting observations of sociability was only partially satisfactory.

> In short, December of 1955 found us under orders to bring back the "inside dope," remaining outsiders looking in. We could not do it?

> Eventually, we decided that the only solution was to draw on our own sociable contacts, extending the range of our sociable activity, soliciting and accepting invitations from persons whom we knew only slightly, using brokers to introduce us to parties where we might not otherwise be asked, and in general using whatever resources were available to us as individuals for maximizing the range of our sociable experiences.

An equally compelling example of serendipity in the data collection process is offered by John Van Maanen in an article on police socialization in the *Administrative Science Quarterly* (1975: 209):

> Each recruit group represented a different stage in the formal socialization process. Originally, the study was designed to approximate a modified version of Solomon's . . . four-fold group design, but certain unpredictable circumstances intervened to prevent this more rigorous design. For example: training facilities became overcrowded and one group was prevented from following its planned sequence; maintenance of good will between the researcher and the Department required that cer-

tain changes be made in the study design; training policies were altered after the research was begun; and so on. However, the operational difficulties were of minor importance since the major research problem, access, had already been solved.

In the face of such apparent chaos in the data collection process, it is relatively easy to become discouraged, cynical, or even fatalistic. Hence, as a partial antidote for such feelings, consider a less pessimistic viewpoint on this state of affairs offered several years ago by Howard Becker (1965: 602-603):

> As every researcher knows, there is more to doing research than is dreamt of in philosophies of science, and texts in methodology offer answers to only a fraction of the problems one encounters. The best laid research plans run up against unforeseen contingencies in the collection and analysis of data; the data one collects may prove to have little to do with the hypothesis one sets out to test; unexpected findings inspire new ideas. No matter how carefully one plans in advance, research is designed in the course of its execution. The finished monograph is the result of hundreds of decisions, large and small, made while the research is under way and our standard texts do not give us procedures and techniques for making these decisions. . . .
> I must take issue with one point: . . . that social research being what it is, we can never escape the necessity to improvise, the surprise of the unexpected, our dependence on inspiration. . . .
> It is possible, after all, to reflect on one's difficulties and inspirations and see how they could be handled more rationally the next time around. In short, one can be methodical about matters that earlier had been left to chance and improvisation and thus cut down the area of guesswork.

In essence, it is this very possibility of becoming more methodical about matters that in previous research have been left largely to idiosyncrasy, circumstance, or inspiration that constitutes the major reason for reviewing these many examples of choices and constraints in the social research process. If the existing methodological decision process is to be improved, it is essential that we describe and explain that process as accurately as we can. That description must take into account the fact that methodological choices are not made in a way that conforms very well to the ideal process implied in our research literature and conventional textbooks on methods. In Broedling's (1975: 4) words, "increasing methodological self-awareness is a necessary prerequisite to deciding what improvements can and should be made," and, in our view, the systematic accumulation of candid descriptions of how behavioral and social science research is actually conducted will prove to be a valuable component in our efforts to become more methodological about idiosyncrasies of person and circumstances in the research enterprise.

REFERENCES

BABBIE, E. R. (1979) The Practice of Social Research. Belmont, CA: Wadsworth.

BECKER, H. S. (1965) "Review of P. E. Hammond's Sociologists at Work." American Sociological Review 30: 602-603.

BELL, C. and H. NEWBY (1977) Doing Sociological Research. New York: Macmillan.

BLAU, J. R. and W. McKINLEY (1979) "Ideas, complexity, and innovation." Administrative Science Quarterly 24: 200-219.

BLAU, P. M. (1964) "The dynamics of bureaucracy," in P. E. Hammond (ed.) Sociologists at Work. New York: Basic Books.

——— (1955) The Dynamics of Bureaucracy. Chicago: University of Chicago Press.

BRICKMAN, P. (1980) Personal communication (interview, August).

BROEDLING, L. A. (1975) "Methodological Choice," in H. W. Sinaiko and L. A. Broedling (eds.) Perspectives on Attitude Assessment: Surveys and Their Alternatives. Champaign, IL: Pendleton.

BROWNE, J. (1976) "Fieldwork for fun and profit," in M. P. Golden (ed.) The Research Experience. Itasca, IL: Peacock.

CAMERON, K. (1978) "Measuring organizational effectiveness in institutions of higher education." Administrative Science Quarterly 23: 604-632.

CHAMPOUX, J. E. (1980) "A three sample test of some extensions to the job characteristics model of work motivation." Academy of Management Journal 23, 3: 466-478.

CORNELIUS, E. T. and K. S. LYNESS (1980) "A comparison of holistic and decomposed judgment strategies in job analyses by job incumbents." Journal of Applied Psychology 65, 2: 155-163.

DAFT, R. L. and P. J. BRADSHAW (1980) "The process of horizontal differentiation: two models." Administrative Science Quarterly 25: 441.

DAVIS, J. A. (1964) "Great books and small groups: an informal history of a national survey," in P. E. Hammond (ed.) Sociologists at Work. New York: Basic Books.

——— (1961) Great Books and Small Groups. New York: Free Press.

DOSSETT, D. L., G. P. LATHAM, and L. M. SAARI (1980) "The impact of goal setting on survey returns." Academy of Management Journal 23, 3: 561-567.

GANS, H. (1962) Urban Villagers. New York: Macmillan.

GELLER, E. S., J. F. WITMER, and M. A. TUSO (1977) "Environmental interventions for litter control." Journal of Applied Psychology 62, 3: 344-351.

GOLDEN, M. P. (1976) The Research Experience. Itasca, IL: Peacock.

GRELLER, M. M. (1980) "Evaluation of feedback sources as a function of role and organizational level." Journal of Applied Psychology 65, 1: 24-27.

HACKMAN, J. R. (1980) Personal communication (interview, August).

HAMMOND, P. E. (1964) Sociologists at Work: Essays on the Craft of Social Research. New York: Basic Books.

HOROWITZ, I. L. (1969) Sociological Self-images: A Collective Portrait. Beverly Hills, CA: Sage.

HYMAN, H. H., C. R. WRIGHT, and T. K. HOPKINS (1962) Application of Methods of Evaluation: Four Studies of the Encampment for Citizenship. Berkeley: University of California Press.

KANTER, R. M. (1980) Interview conducted by B. A. Stein (September).

——— (1977) Men and Women of the Corporation. New York: Basic Books.

——— and B. A. STEIN (1979) Life in Organizations: Workplaces as People Experience Them. New York: Basic Books.

KAPLAN, A. (1964) The Conduct of Inquiry. San Francisco: Chandler.

KATZ, D. (1980) Personal communication (interview, July).

KELMAN, II. C. (1972) "The rights of the subject in social research: an analysis in terms of relative power and legitimacy." American Psychologist 27, 11: 989-1016.

LEEGE, D. C. and W. L. FRANCIS (1974) Political Research: Design, Measurement, and Analysis. New York: Basic Books.

MARTIN, J. (1981) "A garbage can model of the research process." Presented at the Conference on Innovations in Methodology for Organizational Research, Greensboro, N.C., March.

MATTHEWS, D. R. (1971) "From the Senate to simulation," in O. Walter (ed.) Political Scientists at Work. Belmont, CA: Wadsworth.

McCARTHY, J. D. and M. B. McCARTHY (1975) "Power and Purpose in survey research (If you got the money, honey, I got the time)," in G. H. Lewis (ed.) Fistfights in the Kitchen. Pacific Palisades, CA: Goodyear.

McGRATH, J. E. (1981) "Dilemmatics: the study of choices and dilemmas in the research process." Presented at the Conference on Innovations in Methodology for Organizational Research, Greensboro, N.C., March.

McKELVEY, B. and R. H. KILMAN (1975) "Organization design: a participative multivariate approach." Administrative Science Quarterly 20: 24-36.

MOORE, R. (1977) "Becoming a sociologist in Parkwood," in C. Bell and H. Newby (eds.) Doing Sociological Research. New York: Macmillan.

PLATT, J. (1976) Realities of Social Research. New York: John Wiley.

REX, J. and R. MOORE (1967) Race, Community, and Conflict. Oxford: Oxford University Press.

REISMAN, D. and J. WATSON (1964) "The sociability project: a chronicle of Frustration and achievement," in P. E. Hammond (ed.) Sociologists at Work. New York: Basic Books.

TANNENBAUM, A. S. (1980) Personal communication (interview, August).

—— B. KAVCIC, M. ROSNER, M. VIANELLO, and G. WIESER (1974) Hierarchy in Organizations: An International Comparison. San Francisco: Jossey-Bass.

TROW, M. (1957) "Comment on 'Participant observation and interviewing: a comparison.'" Human Organization 16: 33-35.

VAN MAANEN, J. (1975) "Police socialization: a longitudinal examination of job attitudes in an urban police department." Administrative Science Quarterly 207-228.

WALTER, O. (1971) Political Scientists at Work. Belmont, CA: Wadsworth.

WILSON, M. (1978) Social and Educational Research in Action: A Book of Readings. London: Longman.

WRIGHT, C. R. and H. H. HYMAN (1964) "The evaluators," in P. E. Hammond (ed.) Sociologists at Work. New York: Basic Books.

3

Dilemmatics
The Study of Research Choices and Dilemmas

Joseph E. McGrath

☐ The research process can be viewed as a *series of interlocking choices,* in which we try *simultaneously to maximize several conflicting desiderata.* Viewed in that way, the research process is to be regarded not as a set of problems to be "solved," but rather as a set of dilemmas to be "lived with"; and the series of interlocking choices is to be regarded not as an attempt to find the "right" choices but as an effort to keep from becoming impaled on one or another horn of one or more of these dilemmas.

From this perspective—from this "dilemmatic view of the research process"—a proper starting place for a discussion of methodology is: (a) to lay out the series of generic choice points; (b) to describe those choices in "dilemmatic" terms—that is, in terms of the mutually incompatible goals involved, and in terms of the dilemmatic consequences involved in *any* of the available choices; and then (c) to discuss what the beleaguered researcher can do.

Author's Note: Many of the ideas in this chapter are variations and extensions of ideas presented in Runkel and McGrath (1972). They were developed through fascinating discussions with Philip Runkel, with many graduate students and faculty colleagues at the University of Illinois, and with my workshop teammates, Joanne Martin and Richard Kulka. I am grateful to all of them for helping me gain new understandings of the research process in our field.

The upshot of such a view of research is, of course, rather unpolyanna. Not only is there no one true method, or correct set of methodological choices that will guarantee success; there is not even a "best" strategy or set of choices for a given problem, setting, and available set of resources. In fact, from the dilemmatic point of view, *all research strategies and methods are seriously flawed,* often with their very strengths in regard to one desideratum functioning as serious weaknesses in regard to other, equally important, goals. Indeed, *it is not possible, in principle, to do "good"* (that is, methodologically sound) *research.* And, of course, to do good research, *in practice,* is even harder than that. (We are a very long way from converting "dilemmatics" into "dilemmetrics," much less into a full-fledged "dilemmatology." And there is no "dilemmagic" that will make the problems go away!)

A first confrontation with the dilemmatic view of research often leaves one very pessimistic, not only about the state of the art of the field, but also about the value of that particular field. Dilemmatics is certainly not a polyanna philosophy. It is extremely skeptical, though it need not be cynical. I regard it as *realistic,* rather than pessimistic. I see no merit at all in pretending that our methods can deliver what we wish they could but know they cannot, namely, to provide noncontingent certainty unperturbed by the methods of study and unperturbed over time! Perhaps someone might want to make a case for trying to fool sponsors, agencies, or clients, in regard to what our methods can and cannot do. But there is no rationale at all, I believe, for trying to fool ourselves in these matters. This point leads directly to a statement of the First and Second Rules of Dilemmatics:

RULE I: Always *face* your methodological problems squarely; or, Never turn your back on a Horned-Dilemma.

RULE II: A wise researcher never rests; or,
That laurel you are about to sit on may turn out to be an unrecognized horn of another methodological dilemma.

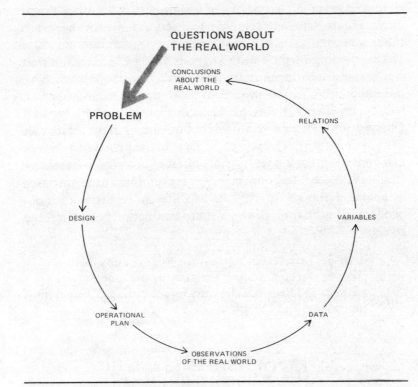

QUESTIONS ABOUT
THE REAL WORLD

CONCLUSIONS
ABOUT THE
REAL WORLD

PROBLEM

RELATIONS

DESIGN

VARIABLES

OPERATIONAL
PLAN

DATA

OBSERVATIONS
OF THE REAL WORLD

Figure 3.1 The Cycle of Empirical Research
SOURCE: Runkel and McGrath, 1972.

STRATEGIES, DESIGNS, AND METHODS
AS STAGES OF THE RESEARCH PROCESS

We can regard the research process as a series of logically ordered—though chronologically chaotic—choices. Those choices run from formulation of the problem, through design and execution of a study, through analysis of results and their interpretation. *The series of choices is locally directional:* Plan must come before execution; data collection must come before data analysis. *But the set of choices is systemically circular:* It starts with a problem, and gets back to the problem. The end result of the process, however, never arrives back at the exact starting point, even if all goes well. So, the process really should be regarded as a series of spirals, rather than as a closed circle. Figure 3.1 illustrates this, and sets a frame for the rest of this material.

The labeling of the figure suggests that we can divide that circle/spiral into meaningful "chunks." This chapter will give minimum attention to several of those stages. Main attention will be on stages involving Design, Operational Plans, and Observations. One can state a set of dilemmas and a related set of choices within each of these "stages" of the problem. Choices and consequences are really quite interconnected across stages. In spite of those interconnections, it is useful for some purposes to act as if the set of choices at different levels were independent. This chapter draws a sharp distinction between three levels:

(a) strategies or research settings for gaining knowledge;
(b) plans or research designs for carrying out studies; and
(c) methods or research techniques for measuring, manipulating, controlling, and otherwise contending with variables.

RESEARCH STRATEGIES AND THE THREE-HORNED DILEMMA

CLASSES OF STRATEGIES

Methodological strategies are generic classes of research settings for gaining knowledge about a research problem. There are (at least) eight readily distinguishable research strategies (see Figure 3.2). They are related to each other in intricate ways, some of which are reflected in Figure 3.2. They can be viewed as eight "pie slices" within a circumplex; but also as four quadrants, each with a related pair of strategies. The circular space is defined in terms of two orthogonal axes: (a) the use of obtrusive versus unobtrusive operations, and (b) concern with universal or generic behavior systems versus concern with particularistic or concrete behavior systems. But

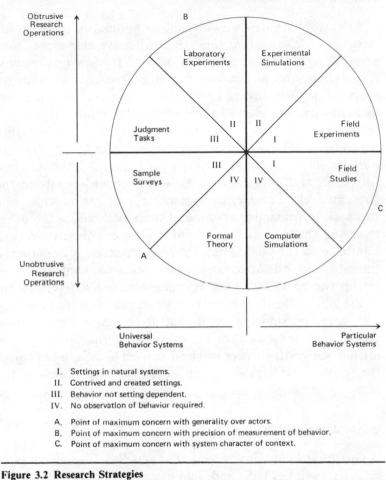

I.   Settings in natural systems.
II. Contrived and created settings.
III. Behavior not setting dependent.
IV. No observation of behavior required.

A.   Point of maximum concern with generality over actors.
B.   Point of maximum concern with precision of measurement of behavior.
C.   Point of maximum concern with system character of context.

Figure 3.2 Research Strategies
SOURCE: Runkel and McGrath, 1972.

within that two-dimensional space there are three "maxima,"
points at which each of three mutually conflicting desiderata
are realized at their highest values (marked A, B, and C in the
figure, and to be discussed presently). Thus, the "2-space"
circumplex maps the territory of a *three-horned dilemma*!

THREE CONFLICTING DESIDERATA

All research evidence involves some population (here, A, for Actors) doing something (here, B, for Behavior) in some time/place/thing setting (here C, for Context). It is *always desirable (ceteris paribus) to maximize:* (A) *generalizability* with respect to populations, (B) *precision* in control and measurement of variables related to the behavior(s) of interest, and (C) existential *realism,* for the participants, of the context within which those behaviors are observed. But, alas, *ceteris is never paribus,* in the world of research. In Figure 3.2, the maxima for A, B, and C are shown at widely spaced points in the strategy circle. The very choices and operations by which one can seek to maximize any one of these will reduce the other two; and the choices that would "optimize" on any two will minimize on the third. Thus, the research strategy domain is a three-horned dilemma, and *every* research strategy either avoids two horns by an uneasy compromise but gets impaled, to the hilt, on the third horn; or it grabs the dilemma boldly by one horn, maximizing on it, but at the same time "sitting down" (with some pain) on the other two horns. Some of these dilemmatic consequences will be discussed later, as we examine the research strategies in each of the four quadrants of the strategy circumplex.

QUADRANT I STRATEGIES

Quadrant I contains two familiar and closely related strategies: field studies (FS) and field experiments (FX). Both are characterized by—and distinguished from the other six strategies by—taking place in settings that are existentially "real" for the participants. They differ in that field studies are as unobtrusive as they can be, while field experiments are a one-step compromise toward obtrusiveness in the interest of increasing precision with respect to behavior, B. Note that desideratum C (realism of context) is at a maximum in the field study octant. However, both desideratum B (precision with regard to measurement, manipulation, and control of behavior variables) and desideratum A (generalizability with regard to populations) are far from their maxima. The field study, thus, seizes the "C" horn of the dilemma boldly, but must "sit" upon relatively uncomfortable levels of the "A" and "B" horns. (This is no mere hyperbole: To *lack* precision and generalizability is a serious matter even if you *have* realism.)

QUADRANT II STRATEGIES

Quadrant II contains two other familiar research strategies: laboratory experiments (LX) and experimental simulations (ES) (the latter not to be confused with computer simulations, which are to be considered in Quadrant IV). The Quadrant II strategies are distinguished from the Quadrant I strategies in that they involve deliberately contrived settings, *not* existentially "real" for the participants. They differ from each other in that laboratory experiments reflect an attempt to create a generic or universal "setting" for the operation of the behavior processes under study, while experimental simulations reflect an attempt to retain some realism of *content* (what has been called "mundane realism"), even though they have given up realism of *context*. (Whether this is a worthwhile attempt to compromise is a matter for argument, as is the chance of actually attaining "realism.")

Note that the octant of the laboratory experiment contains the point of "maximum" for desideratum B (precision with regard to measurement of behavior), although it is a very low point with respect to desiderata A and C. Note, also, that the experimental simulation octant, along with the neighboring field experiment octant, lies in between the B and C maxima— neither very high nor very low on either of them. But, at the same time, those octants lie as far as possible from the maximum for desideratum A (generalizability with regard to populations). Thus, these strategies fit snugly between horns B and C, but get fully impaled on the A horn. So: The field study maximizes C (realistic context) but is very low on A and B; and the laboratory experiment maximizes B (precision) but is very low on A and C; field experiments and experimental simulations are moderately high on B and C, but disastrously low on A.

THE THREE-HORNED DILEMMA

These unintended, and often unattended, consequences of choices of research strategies begin to give substance to our earlier remark that, from the "dilemmatic" view of the research process, the very strengths of each strategy, plan, or method with respect to one desideratum is often its main weakness with respect to another desideratum. To maximize on one desideratum (boldly grabbing that horn) is to have relatively unfavorable levels of the other two (that is, to get part way impaled on both of the other two horns). Conversely, to optimize between two desiderata (snugly fitting between those two horns) is to guarantee a minimum on the third desideratum (that is, to get impaled, to the hilt, on the third horn).

There is no way—in principle—to maximize all three (conflicting desiderata of the research strategy domain. Stating that stark principle leads to formulation of the third rule of Dilemmatics:

RULE III: The researcher, like the voter, often must choose the lesser among evils.

While it is not possible to avoid these choices many researchers dream of doing so. Such dreams are fantasies, and that suggests a statement of the Fourth Rule of Dilemmatics:

RULE IV: It is *not possible, in principle,* to do an unflawed study; or,

Fantasize, if you will, about lying in clover, but be prepared to awake on a bed of horns.

QUADRANT III STRATEGIES

The pair of research strategies located in Quadrant III—the sample survey (SS) and the judgment study (JS)—are contrasted with both the Quadrant I and the Quadrant II strategies in regard to both context and population sampling. Quadrant I deals with behavior in a "real" context—one that exists for the participants independently of the study and its purposes. Quadrant II deals with a contrived context, but deals with behavior as it occurs within—and intrinsically connected to— that context. In other words, for laboratory experiments and experimental simulations, the context has *experimental* reality though not *existential* reality for the participants. In Quadrant III, it is the intent of the investigator that the context should *not* play a part in the behavior of concern. In the case of judgment studies, the investigator tries to mute or nullify context—by "experimental control" of "all" extraneous conditions at what the investigator hopes will be neutral or innocuous levels. In the case of sample surveys, the investigator tries to neutralize context by asking for behaviors (often, responses to questions) that are unrelated to the context within which they are elicited (often, doorstep or telephone).

In regard to population sampling: Quadrant I studies are stuck with the "real" populations that already inhabit the settings studied; and Quadrant II studies often are stuck with whatever participants they can lure to the lab. The two strategies of Quadrant III both take sampling far more seriously, but in two different ways. The sample survey maximizes concern with effective sampling of the population units to be studied (be they individuals, or organizations, or dyads, or other social units). The judgment study typically uses only a few population units—construed as "judges" of stimuli, not as "respondents" to stimuli—presumably under the assumption that those judges are somehow "generic" judges. But at the same time, judgment studies typically focus much care on appropriate sampling—usually systematic rather than representative sampling of the stimuli to which the judges are to respond.

The judgment study (like the experimental simulation) is an uneasy compromise between two desiderata (B and A) with desideratum C (realism of context) at a minimum. The sample survey maximizes A (population generalizability), but does so by buying relatively low levels of B (precision) and C (realism of context). Judgment studies sit down hard on the C horn of the dilemma, while snuggling moderately between the A and B horns. Sample surveys deal effectively with the A horn, but rest uncomfortably, partly impaled on the other two (B and C) horns.

QUADRANT IV STRATEGIES

The two strategies of Quadrant IV differ from the strategies of the other three quadrants in that they are *not empirical.* There are no Actors. No Behavior occurs. There is no behavior Context. Rather, these two strategies are *theoretical.* One, here called formal theory (FT), refers to all attempts at general theory—in the sense of universal versus particular, but not necessarily in the sense of broad versus narrow content. The other, computer simulations (CS), refers to all attempts to *model* a particular concrete system (or set of concrete systems) —not necessarily using a computer, or even formal mathematics, though such is almost always the case in actuality. Formal theories, like sample surveys, maximize population generalizability (A) though they are quite low on realism of context (C) and on precision of measurement (B). Computer simulations (like experimental simulations and judgment studies) are compromises that try to optimize two desiderata (A and C), but do so at the price of minimizing the third (B). Thus, as with the empirical strategies, these theoretical strategies require either handling one "horn" well but sitting on the other two, or fending off two horns while paying a price on the third. That state of affairs suggests the Fifth Rule of Dilemmatics:

RULE V: You can't build flawless theory, either; or,
          You have to be careful about dilemma horns even
          when you sit down in your theoretical armchair.

SOME CONCLUDING COMMENTS ABOUT RESEARCH STRATEGIES

Many discussions of research strategies are carried out in terms of a much smaller set of strategies, often only two: lab versus field, survey versus lab, lab versus field study versus field experiment, empirical versus theoretical, or experiment versus simulation (meaning, variably, either experimental simulation or computer simulation). Furthermore, the set of strategies that is discussed is often a mixed bag (from the present point of view) of strategies, designs, and methods. For example, the set might include: lab experiment versus natural observation versus questionnaires; or case studies versus surveys versus correlational studies (meaning studies using archival data); or simply laboratory experiments versus correlation studies (meaning, variously, field studies, surveys, or uses of archival data). It is important, I think, to make explicit all of the classes of strategies, so that we can consider their relations to one another. It is also important, I think, to draw clear distinctions between strategies or settings, study designs, and methods of measurement/manipulation/control. Those different levels or domains of the research process are beset by different problems, or dilemmas; they demand different kinds of choices, and they offer different kinds of alternatives from among which to choose. It is not that they are independent, those different domains; it is just that they are different.

Another problem with many discussions of research strategies is that they proceed from a shaky syllogism. That syllogism goes as follows: "I can point out numerous flaws, indeed fatal flaws, in strategy A (which I am opposing). Since strategy A is bad, therefore strategy B (which I am touting) must be good." It is relatively easy, for example, to point out the many limitations and flaws—indeed fatal flaws, if you like—in laboratory experiments. But if lab experiments are "bad," it does *not* follow that some other strategy (most often Field Studies, occasionally one of the other classes of strategies) must, therefore, be "good." One can equally easily point out the flaws, some fatal, of field studies or of any of the other strategies. Doing so does not make lab experiments "good," either. Indeed, what is the case—and this is the central message of the dilemmatic viewpoint—is that *all* research strategies are "bad" (in the sense of having serious methodological limitations); none of them are "good" (in the sense of being even relatively unflawed). So, methodological discussions should not waste time arguing about which is the right strategy, or the best one; they are *all* poor in an absolute sense. Instead, such discussions might better engage in questions of how best to *combine* multiple strategies (*not within* one study, but over studies within a program) so that information can be gained about a given problem by *multiple means that do not share the same weaknesses*. This central theme—of using multiple methodological probes to gain sustantive convergence by methods that compensate for one another's vulnerabilities—will occur again in discussion of the other two levels, design and methods.

DILEMMAS IN RESEARCH DESIGN

DESIGNS, VALIDITIES, AND THREATS TO VALIDITY

Several classifications are relevant at the design level. Campbell and his colleagues have done the definitive work here (see

Campbell and Stanley, 1966; Cook and Campbell, 1979; Webb et al., 1966). First, they offer a classification of designs into preexperimental (3), true experimental (3), and quasi-experimental (17). Second, they describe four kinds of validity—internal, statistical conclusion, construct, and external. Third, they provide a list of major classes of threats to each of those types of validity: that is, they list classes of plausible rival hypotheses. Put together, these constitute a 23 (designs) by 32 (classes of threats to validity, nested with four types of validity) Campbellian matrix, that represents a definitive treatment of research design at this level of analysis. Thorough familiarity with the Campbellian 23 x 32 matrix is assumed throughout the rest of this material.

COMPARISON VERSUS CORRELATION

Another familiar distinction, related to the Campbellian classification of designs, is the distinction between "experimental" and "correlational" studies (see Cronbach, 1957). The first refers to designs that *compare average values of different batches of cases* (relative to variation in values *within* each batch) *on some attribute.* The second refers to designs that *examine the covariation of the values of two or more attributes,* among the cases of a *single batch.* Actually, the two are ultimately convertible, one to the other, since they are each special cases of the same, underlying Baconian logic-of-relations between events or properties of events: If X goes with Y, and X[1] goes with Y[1], invariably, then, X and Y are related. If I have reason to believe that X comes first, and/or that X is not affected by Y, and that all other pertinent matters are taken into account (all other attributes are controlled, or otherwise eliminated), then I can infer that X led to Y, or that X is a necessary and/or sufficient condition for Y, or that X "causes" Y.

Correlational designs (assuming relatively sophisticated ones, of course) are very good for finding out the functional form of the X-Y relation (e.g., linear, curvilinear); for specifying value mapping between X and Y (how many units of increase in X will yield one unit of increase in Y?); and for determining the degree of predictability of Y from X (i.e., the size of the correlation). But correlational designs are blunt instruments, relatively speaking, for interpreting the causal direction, if any, of the X-Y relation. Experimental or comparison designs have precisely the opposite virtues and weaknesses. Good experimental designs are excellent for examining the causal nexus by which X and Y are connected. But they are seldom useful in assessing the functional form, or the value mappings of X on Y, and they give only quite constrained and contingent information about degree of predictability of Y from X. This set of contrasts points to some major dilemmas in the design domain, ones that can be examined better if we first consider some further classifications at a more microlevel.

REPLICATION AND PARTITIONING

A single observation is not science.

All research requires multiple observations, though not necessarily multiple "cases." Case studies use only one population unit—one "A" unit in the symbol system we are using here. But they involve extensive observation of that one case.

All research requires some form of *aggregation* of those observations. So-called "qualitative" studies involve multiple observations of one or more "cases"—whether or not the observations are then mapped via numbers into magnitudes, order relations, or frequencies. And those observations must be aggregated in *some* way before they can be interpreted— whether or not that aggregation is done on some simple and explicit basis, such as an average, or on some complex and more implicit basis, such as pattern expressed in words rather than in numbers.

The researcher is always and continually faced with deciding how to aggregate such multiple observations. While it is literally true that no two observations are identical, the researcher must decide which sets of two or more observations are to be treated *as if* the observations in the set were all alike (that is, to decide which observations will be treated as "replications"); and which two or more sets of observations are to be treated as if the sets were different (that is, which sets will be treated as "partitions" across which comparisons can be made).

In correlating X with Y, for example, the researcher decides to treat each individual "case" as different; but at the same time, decides that each individual was the "same" person when data were collected for attribute X and when data were collected for attribute Y—even if those observational events occurred years apart, and even if those events varied greatly, in time and context, from one case to the next.

In comparison studies, the investigator decides that all cases within a given condition are to be considered "the same" replications—not literally true, of course—and that the different sets of observations defined by the different combinations of experimental conditions will be treated as different—as meaningful partitions of the data set. These same and difference decisions, these replication and partitioning choices, go on at several levels. They occur, for example, when we aggregate items within a single test. If we score a 30-item test by calculating number correct, varying from 0 to 30, we are implicitly treating the 30 items as replications. If, instead, we identify two factors (by whatever means, theoretical or empirical), one with 19 items and the other with 11 items, and compute two separate scores, we are partitioning that set of 30 observations into *two batches* that we will treat as different (although we are still treating all 19 items in one batch and all 11 items in the other as replications). We also make such replication and partitioning decisions when we aggregate over trials or observation periods. We decide which time-ordered sets of observations belong together, and which should be batched separately, and in doing so we are deciding, in effect, which time periods contain meaningfully different situations, or chunks of behavior.

What is important to note here is that such same and different decisions are *arbitrary and tentative*. They are *arbitrary* because any two observations are really alike in some respects and different in others, and it is up to the investigator to decide which of these "respects" are to be focused on. They are *tentative,* or should be regarded as tentative, because it is often useful to take cases treated alike for one purpose and later partition among them for another purpose, and vice versa. Analysis of variance and covariance makes this point well. If one does an analysis of variance, one treats cases within a cell as "alike." If one then adds a covariance analysis, one would be, in effect, partitioning the cases within each cell on that covariate. The reverse change can also be illustrated from ANOVA. When categories of one or more factors, or their interactions, show no differences, it is often useful to combine them—thus treating as "same" what had previously been treated as different. Such replication and partitioning decisions are the processes underlying many other decisions within the research process. Some of these will be examined next.

UNCERTAINTY, NOISE, INFORMATION, AND TREATMENT OF VARIABLES

It is worth examining research design decisions at still another, micro, level. This level has to do with how one actually deals with the various attributes or properties of the events one wants to study. Three questions are pertinent here: (1)

What properties (variables) are relevant to my problem? (2) What should I do in regard to those properties with which I am most concerned? (3) What should I do about all the rest?

What are the properties? In regard to the first question: *All properties* of the events being studied that *can or might vary from one observation to another,* are the proper subject of your concern. That means all of the properties on which you *could* partition the set of observations—and that is an infinite set, or, for practical purposes, might as well be. Each of these potential properties of the set of events can vary—that is, each can take any one of two or more values or levels or states. (In the case of a "continuous" variable, we can regard it as having a very large number of levels with very small differences between levels. As an aside, so-called "qualitative" data can take on only one of two "values" in regard to any one property: "present" or "absent" or, more accurately, "observed" or "not observed." In all other regards, they are like any other observations of any property of an event.)

If we consider a "problem" or a "set of observations" as having a certain number of relevant properties, P (1, 2, 3, . . . P); and if we regard each of them as potentially taking on any one of some specific number of different levels or values, V (with V being potentially a different number for each of the properties), then: The total number of possible combinations of values of properties that can occur—that is the total number of "different" events that can occur—is given by: $[(V_1)(V_2)(V_3) \ldots (V_p)]$. If we simplify, by imagining that all properties have the same number of possible different levels, that expression becomes (V^P). For most problems, where p is substantial, (V^P) is a very large number, even if V is only two.

Research as dealing with information, noise, and uncertainty. If any given event or observation can take on any one of the (V^P) values, that expression is a measure of the Uncertainty in, or the Potential Information in, that problem. $V^P = U$. If we reduce that uncertainty (potential information) in the "problem" by doing a study that establishes a relation between the occurrence of various values of X and the co-occurrence of predictable values of Y, there is a reduction in uncertainty. There are now fewer possible combinations of events that can occur. That reduction in uncertainty, from (V^P) to (V^{P-1}) (a substantial amount if P is large) is a statement of the Information Yield of that study.

On the other hand, if we reduce (V^P) by "eliminating" variables—by experimental control, for example—we reduce the potential information in our set of observations, but we do not reduce the uncertainty in the "real-world" problem. When we do this we then *can find out about less.* That is, there is less potential information in our set of observations, because we have cut the scope (in the hope of gaining precision) and thereby left some of the potential information of the problem outside the scope of our study.

If we reduce the amount of potential information (V^P) within our observations by allowing some properties to vary but ignoring them (that is, by not trying to control them and not measuring them), that amount of potential information will function as "noise," and it will *confound* any "signal" that we might have detected (such as the X-Y relation we are investigating). This, too, does not yield information; but rather it confounds what information could have been learned. More will be said about these matters later.

In what ways can I treat the properties of most interest? In regard to the second question asked at the start of this section: there are *four* things you can do in regard to any one property that is of interest in your study:

(1) You can let a particular property *vary freely,* as it will in nature so to speak, *but measure* what value in takes in each instance.

This is called *Treatment Y* here, and it is what one *must* do in regard to one's dependent variable(s).

(2) You can select cases to include in the set of events—or otherwise arrange the conditions of observation—so that all cases have the *same* (and predetermined) *value* on some particular property. This is called *Treatment K* (for constant) here, and it is what we mean when we talk about holding something constant or experimentally (as opposed to statistically) controlling it.

(3) You can deliberately cause one value of the property to occur for one subset of the sets of observations, and a different (but equally predetermined) value of that property to occur for another subset of those observations. This will be called *Treatment X,* and it is what we mean when we talk about "manipulating" an independent variable.

(4) You can divide cases into two (or more) subsets in such a way that the two sets are made *equal on the average* (though varying within set) on a particular property. This will be called *Treatment M* (for "matching"). It of course can be done for more than two sets (as can Treatment X), and for more than one property (as can Treatment K, Treatment X and Treatment Y). It also can be done for both mean and variance (or, for that matter, for any other parameter of the distribution of that property). But notice that Treatment M requires a prior Treatment Y (vary and measure) on the matching property; and it requires a prior division into subsets (a partitioning) on the basis of some other property than those being matched on, (that is, a prior Treatment X).

These four treatments provide different things regarding "replication" and "partitioning" (see Figure 3.3). For Treatment K, the value of the properties is "same" for all cases within subset, and also is the same for the different subsets. For Treatment X, the value of the property is the same for all cases of each subset, but differs—deliberately, and in a way known in advance—from one subset to another. For M, while the *average* value is made equal for various subsets, the *individual* values can and will vary among the cases *within* subsets. For Y, values of the property can and will vary among cases within each subset, and the average value can and perhaps will differ between subsets. (The latter is often the question you are studying.)

What can be done about the other properties? Given a very large number of potentially relevant properties and limited resources, one can only provide Treatments X, K, Y, and M for a relatively small number of those properties. What can be done about all the others? There are four ways to "treat all other properties"—all those that have not been specifically given Y (measurement), X (manipulation), K (held constant), or M (matching) treatments. Those four ways to treat properties-in-general parallel the four treatments of specific properties. They are shown in Figure 3.4.

Note that in all four of the specific treatments of a property you end up knowing either the value of that property that occurred for each event or the average value that occurred for each subset. In the four "general" treatments of "all other" properties, you end up not knowing what values occurred in any case or in any subset of cases.

Two of the four general treatments are especially notable for present purposes. One is *Treatment Z,* which lets all of the other properties vary freely, but *ignores* them. Unlike the other treatments, all of which offer advantages and disadvantages, *Treatment Z is always bad, and is bad in all respects.* It is an unmitigated bane. Note, also, that Treatment Z is the general case analog of Treatment Y, measurement, and Y is the nearest thing we have to an unmitigated blessing (except for cost).

The other notable general treatment is *Treatment R* (for Randomization). It involves assigning cases to subsets (defined by one or more X-treated or manipulated properties) on a random basis. Treatment R is the *sine qua non* for a "true experiment." But it is by no means an unmixed blessing, much

VALUES OF THE PROPERTY AMONG CASES WITHIN EACH SUBSET	AVERAGE VALUE OF THE PROPERTY BETWEEN CASES IN DIFFERENT SUBSETS	
	Same	*Different*
Same	K	X
Different	M	Y

Figure 3.3 The Four Specific Modes for Treatment of Variables
SOURCE: Runkel and McGrath, 1972.
Mode K: held constant.
Mode X: experimentally manipulated (partitioned).
Mode Y: allowed to vary, and measured.
Mode M: matched, across groups, no specific property.

WHAT DOES THE INVESTIGATOR DO ABOUT THE VARIABLE?	WHAT DOES THE INVESTIGATOR LATER KNOW ABOUT THE VARIABLE?	
	Knows Values for Each Case	*Does Not Know Values*
Makes it constant within subset *and* between subsets	Mode K: design constant	(Unknown sampling constraint)
Makes it constant within subset, but lets it vary between subsets	Mode X: design partition	(Unknown sampling bias)
Lets it vary within subset, but makes it constant between subsets	Mode M: matched groups	Mode R: randomization[a]
Lets it vary within and between subsets	Mode Y: observed partition	Mode Z: ignoring the variable

[a] Randomization does not guarantee equivalent distributions between subsets, as does M, but makes them the most probable outcome of the assignment of cases to subsets.

Figure 3.4 Comparison of Modes for Treatment of Variables
SOURCE: Runkel and McGrath, 1972.

less a panacea for all research design problems. Randomization is crucial, and powerful, but, in spite of its very good press, it is *not Dilemmagic!* Indeed, it is at the core of some dilemmas, as we will see later in this section.

Randomization has at least four major weaknesses:

(1) It cannot always be applied, for technical, practical, and/or ethical reasons (see Cook and Campbell, 1979).

(2) While it renders a number of major classes of threats to internal validity far less plausible (see Campbell and Stanley, 1966), there are several classes of threats to internal validity that are unaffected by randomization (see Cook and Campbell, 1979).

(3) While randomization makes "no difference" the most likely value, for differences (on any one property), between subsets over which cases were randomly assigned, it by no means guarantees no differences on any one property; and one certainly should not expect "no differences between subsets" on *every possible* property, even if you have assigned at random.

(4) While randomization increases the chances of having "no difference" between subsets on each of the "other properties," *it absolutely guarantees having a lot of variations within each subset,* on each and every one of those properties. In fact, the most likely outcome is that each property will vary as widely within each subset as it does in the whole set (taking different sample sizes into account). Note that cases within a subset are to be treated *as if alike* for analysis purposes, and that variation within subset functions as random error or "noise." So, if *any* of these properties have *any* effects on the X-Y relation being examined, then Treatment R will act to increase noise (relative to the X-Y "signal") and thereby to reduce the chances of detecting the X-Y signal even if it is truly "there."

SOME DILEMMAS IN THE DESIGN DOMAIN

These points bring to the fore some of the dilemmas of research design. First, there is the R dilemma. Randomization is both a cure and a curse, a bane and a boon. On the one hand, randomization is costly, does not help reduce certain major threats to internal validity, often poses practical and ethical problems, does not guarantee comparability, and does guarantee high within subset variability (i.e., noise). On the other hand, randomization is *essential,* because without it one cannot disentangle causal connections for the X-Y relation.

The other treatment operations are also dilemmatic in their effects. The treatment operations (X and K) that give you the most logical leverage regarding the X-Y relation, by cutting down "noise," are the very operations that limit the *scope* of the question, so that resulting information is very much constrained. (This has to do with one aspect of external validity.) So, there is a trade-off between scope (the amount of potential information in the problem) and precision (the amount of reduction of noise). On the other hand, the treatment operations (Y and R) that allow broader generalization from results are the very ones that incorporate much "noise" into the information that is contained in the sct of observations, making it hard to detect "signal" if it is there. This is another trade-off between scope (amount of information in the problem) and precision (amount of noise in the information). Together, these pose the researcher with the following choices: You can reduce noise, by cutting scope, so you can learn more about less. Or, you can leave scope broad, by accepting noise along with signal, in which case you can learn less about more. At the limit, if you constrain scope by manipulating and controlling more and more variables, there will be no potential information left, and you will then be able to learn everything about nothing. That is the case, in fact, for the research strategy called Computer Simulations, where there are lots of X and K treatments, and some R treatments, but no Y treatments—thus *no* potential information *at all*. At the other limit, you can constrain less and less—eschewing X and K and M treatments—to maximize scope (and noise), using Y for some variables of interest and Z for all the rest. Here, at the limit, you can learn little or nothing about everything. This is more or less what happens in that research called Field Studies.

The latter dilemma—information versus noise, or scope versus precision—is one instance of a very pervasive set of dilemmas within the research process. The general class of dilemmas can be characterized as *standardization versus generalizability* (which is really replication versus partitioning in disguise!). There is a direct conflict between maximizing two desiderata. (a) On the one hand, it is desirable to maximize *standardization*—of "irrelevant" conditions (time of day, color of walls, and so on), of methods of measurement, and so forth—because from such standardization we hope to *gain precision by reducing noise* (i.e., reducing variations within cell, among cases treated alike). (b) On the other hand, it is equally desirable to maximize the range of conditions over which a relation has been tested—by varying "irrelevant conditions," varying methods of measurement, and the like—because from such heterogeneity we hope to gain increased *generalizability* with regard to those varying properties, and thereby gain heightened confidence in the breadth and robustness of the X-Y relation we are assessing.

There is another dilemma that was suggested but not emphasized earlier in this section on design. It has to do with deciding how many different combinations of conditions are to be compared, and how many cases are to be obtained for each combination of conditions. Again, there is a direct conflict between two desiderata. On the one hand, it is *always desirable to increase the number of levels* of an independent variable whose effect is to be studied; and, indeed, it is desirable to test multiple levels of multiple independent variables (that is, it is desirable to increase the total number of partitions). On the other hand, it is *always desirable to increase the number of cases within each subset,* the number of cases to be treated as replications. The latter gives more stability to our estimate of the average value of each subset, each combination of conditions. The former gives more stability to our estimate of the functional relations between variables, X and Y.

But there is always an upper limit to the total number of cases or observations—an upper limit in principle, as well as in practice, because at some point "new" observations must be viewed as "different from" earlier ones. If we take N as the total number of observations, k as the total number of combinations of conditions, or number of "cells," and m as the number of observations in each "cell," then: It is inexorably the case that

N = km. If there is a fixed N, then any operation that increases either m or k—both of which are desiderata to be maximized—will inevitably decrease the other.

I am sure the reader will see that the four major dilemmas described here—the dilemma of R, the precision versus scope or information versus noise dilemma, the standardization/generalizability dilemma, and the N/k/m dilemma—are really all related to one another, and to the dilemmas of the strategy level (and, it will turn out, to those of the methods level, our next topic). I am sure the reader will also see that, at the heart of all these matters is the Campbellian matrix of designs, forms of validity, and classes of threats to validity. Equally at the heart of these matters if the Cronbachian treatment of the "two disciplines of psychology," experimental and correlational. What is offered here is a dilemmatic view of these matters, one that points to the *inherent limitations of all choices* in the design domain—as well as in the strategy domain and, yet to come, in the method domain. I would hope, with such a view, to discourage the reader from seeking "the right design," either in general or for a particular problem, and encourage him or her, instead, to *accept the inevitable limitations and dilemmas of our methods* as constraints within which we must work, and therefore to set out to do the best we can with what we've got!

DILEMMAS AT THE METHODS LEVEL

The third domain of methods deals with how we can measure, manipulate, control, and otherwise contend with variables. Here we find some ties with what has gone before. For one thing, these map to the treatments of properties discussed under Design. Y treatment is measurement, X is manipulation, K is experimental control, and M, R, and alas, Z are ways of "contending with" other variables. So, we have already said much about these methods. Moreover, we again find a strong Campbellian influence. That is particularly so in regard to the ideas of convergent and discriminant validity, multiple operationalism, and unobtrusive measurement (see Campbell and Fiske, 1959; Webb et al., 1966). That work has had a strong influence on the material to be presented here.

RELIABILITY, VALIDITY, AND GENERALIZABILITY

Psychology has had a long history of concern with the reliability and validity of measures, and that work has led to the unfolding of many complexities in these concepts. While much progress has been made, it is clear that these matters are far from settled. But in spite of all the complications and unsettled issues, some matters are now clear. One of these is the need for multiple operations—in the interest of assessing both reliability and validity. Another is the importance of seeking convergence among measures that differ in their methodological weaknesses. A third is that the same problems and requirements exist with regard to reliability and validity for manipulations of independent variables as for measurement of dependent variables. A fourth is that we cannot determine the validity and reliability of constructs without reference to a network of relations involving those constructs; but we cannot establish the reliability and validity of such relations between constructs without reference to the validity and reliability of the individual constructs. These points suggest that there are some method-level dilemmas to be explored. They also suggest that we might adopt Commoner's second law of ecology as our next rule of Dilemmatics:

RULE VI: You can't do *one* thing.

THE CONSTRUCT VALIDITY DILEMMA

When we want to test the relation between constructs X and Y, we develop an operational definition (x) for construct X, and an operational definition (y) for construct Y; then find some setting in which to test the empirical relation between x

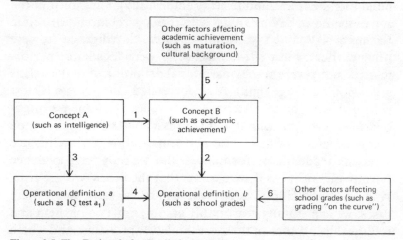

Figure 3.5 The Rationale for Predictive Validity
SOURCE: Runkel and McGrath, 1972.

and y, so that we can draw an inference about X in relation to
Y. There are four relations involved here (see Figure 3.5). One,
X-Y, is conceptual and cannot be tested empirically. Two are
definitional, X-x and Y-y, and they can only be tested indi-
rectly. The fourth is an empirical relation, x-y; and it is used as
the empirical lever by which all three of the others can be
assessed.

If we are hypothesis testing, then what we want to know is
about the conceptual relation; in the example above, (relation
1 in Figure 3.7), X-Y. If so, then we must assume that relations
2 (Y-y) and 3 (X-x) hold, so that we can use relation 4 (x-y) to
test relation 1 (X-Y). If x-y is strong, then (subject to all the
constraints already discussed about design and inference) we
might interpret it as evidence for X-Y. But what if x-y does not
hold? This could occur because x is a poor mapping of X
(relation 3), or y is a poor mapping of Y (relation 2) or because
the x-y data at hand is a poor set of evidence, as well as because
the X-Y conceptual relation does not hold.

If what we had in mind, instead, was to develop a good
measure of X, then one might *do* the same things (build an x,

build or choose a y, and test x-y empirically), but interpret the x-y outcome as having to do with the X-x relation—this time assuming X-Y, and Y-y. Suppose X were "intelligence," x were some particular test of intelligence, Y were "academic performance" and y were some operational definition of that, such as grade point average (gpa). If we correlated scores on an IQ test with gpa and found a strong, positive association, we might conclude favorably about X-x (this is a good IQ test), Y-y (gpa is a good index of academic performance), X-Y (intelligence forecasts academic performance). But we only have evidence for any one of them if we assume that the other two are true. And, since the empirical operations are the same in all these cases, we can equally reasonably assume any two of them and test the third. Which of these we think we are testing, and which we are assuming, is entirely arbitrary and depends on the purposes of the investigator.

One point to make here is that all knowledge is contingent on assumptions. To test something, you must assume some other things; and results of your test hold only to the extent that those assumptions hold. Another point to be made is that construct validation (X-x and Y-y), predictive validity (x-y), and testing theoretical hypotheses (X-Y) are all part of the same enterprise. You are either doing all of them, or none of them. Again, you can't do *one* thing.

CONVERGENT AND DISCRIMINANT VALIDITY

Campbell and Fiske (1959) made it clear more than 20 years ago that we gain validity by means of *convergence* of different measures. It is necessary to have more than one measure of a construct so that the "method variance" associated with any one measure can be separated out. And it is necessary that the multiple measures be of different types, so that the weaknesses of any one type of method can be countervailed by coupling it with other methods that have different weaknesses (Webb et al., 1966). So while multiple operations, all of the same type of method, may help establish reliability, they are not as useful in establishing construct validity. Furthermore, to be confident about our constructs we not only have to establish reliability by correlation of multiple operational definitions of the construct, and establish convergent validity by correlation of different methods of measuring the construct; we also have to establish discriminant validity, showing the boundaries of the construct, by showing *lack* of correlation of measures of the construct with methodologically similar measures of substantively distinct constructs. To know what the construct is (convergent validity) we have to have some knowledge of what it is not (discriminant validity).

This poses another dilemma for the beleaguered researcher, one that is hard to present clearly. It hinges on simultaneously considering convergent and discriminant validity of a construct and hypothesis testing of the relations of that construct with some other construct. When two measures are very similar in form and substance, we tend to think of them as alternative forms of the same measures and, if they correlate highly, regard that as evidence of reliability of that construct. If two measures differ in form but are similar in substance, we might well regard them as alternative measures of the same construct and regard their correlation as evidence of convergent validity. But if two measures differ in substance, we are not altogether sure how to regard them. If they fail to correlate, we might regard that lack of correlation as evidence of discriminant validity of one of the constructs. But if they correlate highly, or even moderately, we might regard that correlation as evidence for a relation between two different constructs, as in substantive hypothesis testing. This set of considerations reminds us that "same" and "different" decisions are made at several levels within the research process, and that they are arbitrary. If two measures are too similar, their high correlation is not remarkable, and is regarded as "merely" a reliability. If two measures are too dissimilar, and they don't correlate, that too is not remarkable, and may be regarded as "merely" evidence of discrimination. But if two measures are different, and they correlate, that is regarded as remarkable, and we often take it to be evidence supporting some substantive hypothesis. This state of affairs is not so much a dilemma as it is a paradox or a quandry. It suggests Dilemmatics Rule 7.

RULE VII: One person's substantive finding is another's method variance.

CLASSES OF MEASURES

Building upon ideas in Webb et al. (1966), Runkel and McGrath (1972) discuss six classes of measures, arrayed on two factors: (a) whether or not the measurement is occurring beknownst to the actor whose behavior is being recorded, and therefore, the extent to which the measure is obtrusive and liable to have reactive effects on the behavior being studied; and (b) whether the behavior record is being made by the actor, by the investigator (or a person or instrument serving as the investigator's surrogate), or by a third party (see Figure 3.6).

Each of the six classes offers strengths and weaknesses. Subjective reports or self-reports—the most popular of the six classes—tempts the researcher to swallow one deadly flaw (reactivity) by wrapping that flaw in several tantalizing strong points (content versatility, low cost, low dross rate, and so on). Trace measures, so attractive in principle because of their unobtrusiveness, are difficult and costly to devise, and often have only a loose coupling to the intended constructs. Observations have a strong appeal as measures of "actual behavior." But observation by a visible observer combines all the reactivity problems of self-reports with some additional observer-based sources of error; while use of hidden observers trades some of those reactivity problems for some practical and ethical—and perhaps legal—problems involved in deceptive strategies. Public records and documents may have a high or low dross rate and cost, and may or may not have problems of reactivity even though they were not recorded as part of a research effort. They resemble trace measures in sometimes

(1) WHO PERFORMS THE BEHAVIOR UNDER STUDY? ALWAYS THE ACTOR.		
	(3) IS THE ACTOR AWARE THAT HIS BEHAVIOR IS BEING RECORDED FOR RESEARCH?	
(2) WHO OBSERVES AND RECORDS THE BEHAVIOR?	*Yes: Observation May Be Reactive*	*No: Observation is Nonreactive*
Actor	Subjective reports	Traces
Researcher	Visible observer	Hidden observer
Recorder in the past	Records of public behavior	Archival records
(4) WHO TRANSLATES RECORDS INTO DATA? ALWAYS THE RESEARCHER.		

Figure 3.6 Sources of Empirical Evidence
SOURCE: Runkel and McGrath, 1972.

being only loosely coupled to the constructs they are used to measure. They can be very valuable, though, when and if appropriate ones are available, because they often offer the best available evidence about very large systems and about the past. Figure 3.7 lists some of the strengths and weaknesses of these six classes of measures.

The central point here, of course, is that one *must use multiple methods, selected from different classes of methods with different vulnerabilities*—not only because this is needed to establish convergent validity, but also because it is needed in order to "finesse" the various threats to validity to which the various classes of methods are vulnerable. The researcher is not posed with a problem of choosing *which one* class of measures to use; the problem is, rather, to choose—and often to devise— a set of measures of each construct that, together, transcend one another's methodological vulnerabilities. This is a problem of creativity and cost, but it is not a true dilemma, since except for cost the desiderata involved (convergence, multiple methods) are not in conflict. After all that has been said in previous pages, it is nice to meet a set of concerns that is "merely" a problem, one that can be solved by increased resources rather than a dilemma that can't be solved at all!

	METHODS OF OBSERVING AND RECORDING					
	Actor's Records		Researcher's Records		Previous Records	
Sources of Invalidity of Methods; That Is, Plausible Rival Hypotheses	*Subjective Reports*	*Trace Measures*	*Visible Observer*	*Hidden Observer*	*Public Behavior*	*Archival Records*
Biases associated with the actor						
1. Guinea pig effect	H		H		M	
2. Role selection	H		H		M	
3. Measurement as change agent	H		H		M	
4. Response sets	H	M	H	M	M	M
Biases associated with the investigator						
5. Effects of interviewer or observer			H	H	M	M
6. Instrument change	H	M	H	H	M	M
Biases associated with the population						
7. Population restrictions	H	H	M	M	M	M
8. Population instability over time	M		M		M	M
9. Population instability among areas	H				M	M
Biases associated with content						
10. Content restrictions		H			M	M
11. Content instability over time		M			H	H
12. Content instability over areas		M			H	H
Other characteristics of methods						
13. Dross rate	H	M	M		M	M
14. Difficulty of access to secondary data	H					
15. Difficulty of replication	H					

KEY: H: High vulnerability to the bias or rival hypothesis.
M: Moderate vulnerability.
Absence of a symbol indicates low vulnerability.

Adapted from Webb and others, 1966.

Figure 3.7 Vulnerabilities of Methods of Observing and Recording

CONCLUDING COMMENTS

This chapter has pointed out some dilemmas—conflicting desiderata—in the strategy, design, and methods domains. It has not said anything about data collection (that is, the actual conduct of the data-getting operations), or data analysis. Some dilemmas are hidden in those domains, too. It also has said little about the interpretation stage, where there are some colossal dilemmas waiting. But enough has been said to make clear the central points of a "dilemmatic" view of research:

(1) The research process teems with dilemmas involving the need to maximize, simultaneously, two or in some cases three conflicting desiderata.

(2) The researcher cannot avoid choosing, nor can he or she find a no-lose strategy, nor a compromise, that does not minimize some other desideratum.

(3) One cannot plan, or execute, flawless research. All strategies, all designs, all methods, are seriously—even fatally—flawed.

(4) No strategy, design, or method *used alone* is worth a damn. Multiple approaches are *required*—at the method level, within study for every construct; at the design and strategy levels, between studies.

(5) Multiple methods not only serve the purposes of replication and convergence; they serve the further, crucial purpose of compensating for inherent limitations that any one method, strategy, or design would have if used alone.

The researcher has a hard and thankless lot! He or she faces a stark set of no-win choices. But the researcher who is fully aware of the dilemmas, who is fully armed with possibilities, can handle the dilemmas. The dilemmas can be handled, *not* by trying to avoid the choices, not by trying to pretend the dilemmas do not exist, certainly not by seeking the "right" choices of strategy, design, and method. They can be handled by bowling them over with multiple methods for all constructs, embedded in multiple designs, using multiple strategies, to gain information about the research problems of concern. We should end this discussion by stating several Final Rules of Dilemmatics, which themselves present one final dilemmatic puzzle:

FINAL RULES: There is no such thing as too much research! There is no such thing as flawless research! But: Poor research is *much worse* than none at all.

The key to that final paradox lies in the dual meanings of good and poor research. We must distinguish between the inherent flaws of any method, when used as well as it can be used, and the quite different matter of using a method badly. The former, the inherent flaws of any method, even when used well, are neither to be decried nor to be overlooked, but rather to be made explicit. The latter—using a method badly— is never acceptable. It is that that is referred to as "poor research" in the final rules. So, while flawless research is not possible, poor research—using potentially valuable-though-flawed methods badly—makes matters worse than they need be. But "good research"—using flawed methods well, and in effective combinations—can help us accrue knowledge about behavioral and social science problems that are of both theoretical and practical concern.

REFERENCES

CAMPBELL, D. T., and J. L. STANLEY (1966) Experimental and Quasi-experimental Design for Research. Skokie, IL: Rand McNally.
COOK, D. T., and D. T. CAMPBELL (1979) Quasi-experimental Design: Design and Analysis Issues for Field Settings. Skokie, IL: Rand McNally.
CRONBACK, L. J. (1957) "The two disciplines of scientific psychology." American Psychologist 12: 671-684.
RUNKEL, P. J., and J. E. McGRATH (1972) Research on Human Behavior: A Systematic Guide to Method. New York: Holt, Rinehart & Winston.
WEBB, E. J., D. T. CAMPBELL, R. D. SCHWARTZ, and L. SECHREST (1966) Unobtrusive Measures: Non Reactive Research in the Social Sciences. Skokie, IL: Rand McNally.

4

Some Quasi-Rules for Making Judgment Calls in Research

Joseph E. McGrath
Joanne Martin
Richard A. Kulka

□ If the actual research process is as chaotic as Martin suggests; if available resources and favorite methods, rather than the nature of the research problem, dominate researchers' decisions, as Kulka's survey indicates; if all methods, even in their idealized forms, are seriously flawed, as McGrath insists—what then is to become of our research enterprise? Should we trade in our worn-out positivistic paradigm, as a number of recent critics have seemed to suggest (although the details of the replacement paradigm are not yet very well specified)? Or should we abandon, altogether, the Baconian, inductive-logic approach to knowledge accrual, reverting to some nonempirical (nonscientific?) approach in our quest for understanding? Or, should we continue working much as we have been—perhaps slaying the messenger who brings the bad news; in any case, discounting if not downright rejecting that bad news—on the grounds that any paradigm

Authors' Note: The material in this chapter grew out of our work together in developing the workshop from which this monograph ensues. It is quite literally an emergent product of our interaction with one another, face to face and via phone and letters, intermittently over the year and a half during which we built the judgment calls work-

that brought the physical sciences this far (i.e., inductive-deductive science) can't be all that bad?

None of these, think we, is the appropriate response.

Rather, we would hold, one ought to take a broader and a more flexible view of what one is engaged in when one is doing research. Research, we maintain, can reasonably be regarded as a knowledge *accrual process.* Many kinds of activities can contribute to that process—some of which we would, and some of which we would not, ordinarily regard as "research." (We argue, later, that activities such as "thinking," "talking to colleagues," "reading in a related area," are all crucial aspects of the knowledge accrual process.) As part of this broader and more flexible view, we need to shift our focus from the individual researcher to the collective research enterprise, and to shift our referent from the method choices of a "next study" to the total stream of intellectual activity bearing on a given problem.

At the same time, we would argue, we should take a more realistic view of what our methods can possibly achieve. If what has been presented in the preceding chapters is at all veridical, the potential contribution of any one method, any one research activity considered in isolation, is very limited indeed. It is only when we have convergent information about the same problem gained from different methods that we can talk of accrual of knowledge. But such an *accrual, of convergent substance from divergent means,*—when and if we can achieve it—is far more robust and generalizable than results of any one study could be. Hence, our view of all methods as limited and flawed can lead to a methodology that offers

---

shop. Therefore, we all three take this opportunity to express our gratitude to each other—for the intellectual excitement, for the interpersonal respect, for the challenging but supportive confrontations about ideas, and for the sheer fun of it! Perhaps we have learned some valuable lessons, not only about the research process, but also about collaboration among colleagues, and perhaps about ourselves.

greater breadth and less vulnerability than what has, thus far, been our practice.

The remainder of this chapter will play and replay those general themes—partly in the form of a set of "quasi-rules"—in order to clarify both where we are today in regard to methodology, and where we can go toward for tomorrow.

THE BACONIAN PARADIGM AND
THE KNOWLEDGE ACCRUAL PROCESS

Baconian induction is a blunt instrument for the accrual of knowledge. Information based on it is *always:* (a) probabilistic, (b) contingent, and (c) requiring cumulation, and these three properties imply some serious limitations to the "knowledge" that can be gained from use of that paradigm. First, we can never know for sure; induction can yield increasing likelihood, but never certainty. Second, we can never know anything independently of the ways we found it out; empirical knowledge is always contingent on the methods, populations, situations, and underlying assumptions involved in the process by which that knowledge was acquired. This is akin to, if not a version of, the Heisenberg uncertainty principle in physics, and it is an everpresent thorn in the side of the behavioral scientist.

From the probabilistic and contingent nature of research we an induce a third property: No one "finding" is evidence, and no one study can yield "knowledge"; empirical information can gain credence *only* by accumulation of convergent results. And from all three of these properties, the probabilistic, contingent and cumulative nature of research information, we can induce an implication that reasonably can be called the fundamental law of the knowledge accrual process: *Knowledge requires convergence of substantive findings derived from a diversity of methods of study.* This is, of course, a restatement of what Campbell and Fiske (1959) told us many years ago. We believe it to be a fundamental feature of scientific method in the social and behavioral sciences.

IDEAL CASE VERSUS ACTUAL RESEARCH

If what we have said before is more or less accurate, then it is impossible, *in principle,* to do flawless research. One cannot, simultaneously, maximize two or more conflicting desiderata. Moreover, in principle, any method—at strategy, design, or measurement levels—has serious flaws. One cannot do research that matches the ideal case!

This should neither surprise nor discourage us. Ideal cases usually cannot be achieved in real-world practice. Ideal cases are "ideal" precisely because they are extreme, limiting cases, defining hypothetical upper levels of attainment. We strive toward, but do not really expect to reach, such upper-limit goals.

Consider, for example, the ideal case definition of reliability of a measure: Agreement of two measurements of the "same" set of "objects," at the "same" time, using the "same" instrument, but carried out so that the two sets are "experimentally independent." That definition, of course, specifies a set of circumstances that is impossible to achieve *in principle.* We cannot measure the same things at the same time with the same instrument and have those measures experimentally independent of one another. When we set about developing information about reliability in practice, we *relax* one or another of those quite stringent requirements: the "sameness" of the time for test/retest, the "sameness" of the instrument for alternate forms, and so forth. We never obtain the ideal-case reliability. But, over successive studies, each relaxing different requirements, we can cumulate reliability information that approaches —but does not ever reach—the ideal case.

So it is with the conduct of research. We cannot do ideal-case research. But we can do research that sets aside one or another requirement or desideratum, then do more research that sets aside different requirements, but fulfills those that were not met in the first study, and so forth. In this way, we can accumulate evidence that is, progressively, less constrained by method limits, more closely approaching—but never reaching —the ideal state. *We should seek not perfection in the single study, but accumulation over studies, using diverse means.*

KNOWLEDGE ACCRUAL AS A CONTINUING PROCESS

No study is ever the first step in the knowledge accrual process, and no study is ever the final step either. The cup of knowledge about a particular question is never really empty, but it is never really full either. There is a flip side to the idea that accumulation over studies is required for empirical information to gain credence. It is the idea that no one study needs to (or can) carry the full burden of determining the final answer to some question. One study can add to our knowledge, but it is not knowledge in and of itself, standing alone.

The foregoing makes some assumptions about what a study is, or, more accurately, about what constitutes a step in the knowledge accrual process. *Many forms of intellectual endeavor can contribute to the knowledge accrual process.* Among them are such activities as thinking, talking to colleagues, reading past research literature, sometimes reading past nonresearch literature, including novels and poetry, becoming knowledgeable in a related area (from which vantage point ideas, analogies, discrepancies, may be noted), reanalyzing data. Each of these formal and informal activities can reasonably be regarded as steps in the knowledge accrual process—surrogate studies, if you will. It is in that light that we argue that no study is the first step, or the last step, in our knowledge accrual about a given program.

CHOOSING AMONG METHODS:
COMPLEMENTARITY NOT REDUNDANCY

We have used the term "method" at several levels—
strategies, designs, and techniques for measuring, manipulating, or controlling variables. At all of these levels, every
method is flawed. But each is flawed differently. Moreover,
each method offers some potential value, as well as some
inherent limitations and some opportunity costs. In many
cases, the very strengths of a method are the seeds of its greatest
weakness. Strategies that yield precision, such as the laboratory experiment, for example, also yield narrow scope and low
realism. Measures that offer one kind of rigor, such as paired
comparison judgments, often are highly reactive. Data analysis
methods that give "strong" answers, such as multiple regres-
sion analyses, do so by imposing many and strong assumptions; hence, the methods themselves strongly determine the
answers.

When we choose among methods at any of the levels (stategy
design, measurement, and the like), therefore, we ought not
regard that task as a search for the "right" answer, but rather
as a choice among complementary possibilities, all of which
are flawed. In research, as in politics, we often must choose
among the lesser of evils, so to speak. With methods, we often
need to choose on the basis of which alternative will make
us least vulnerable, or vulnerable on those aspects we can most
afford to risk. This often turns out to indicate not what is the
best choice, but certain choices that are clearly poor ones
(under the given circumstances). We will elaborate further on
the idea of specifying the "best next step" and/or the "worst
next step" a bit later in the chapter.

In this discussion of good and bad methods, though, it is
important to distinguish between two quite different situations: (a) the inherent flaws of *any* method, even when that
method is applied as well as possible; and (b) the quite different
matter of simply using a method badly. The latter is never

acceptable, and it is such poor use of (potentially good though imperfect) methods to which McGrath alludes when he says that "poor research is worse than none at all." At the same time, we must be careful not to blame the method itself for its misuse. Never throw out a method just because someone has used it badly! But the former situation—recognition that there are inherent flaws of every method, even when well used—is not a matter to be decried. Rather, such weaknesses of methods are to be made explicit, so that they can be compensated for with other, complementary methods, in subsequent research.

We arrive again, therefore, at the fundamental law of the knowledge accrual process: Knowledge accrual requires convergence of findings derived from divergent methods. The method choices are among flawed alternatives. The key element of such choices is to use, next, methods that *complement* (rather than *reproduce*) the weaknesses and strengths of what has been done before.

We hypothesize that the next step in the knowledge accrual process should be as methodologically distant as possible from methods used in prior research on that same problem. *Effective triangulation,* we suggest, *requires distance between the observation posts.* So the best choice for a next step in the knowledge accrual process is a method that has as its strength(s) what the dominant methods used to gather the body of knowledge up to that time have as their major weakness(es). It is desirable, also, that the method chosen for the next step have weaknesses that are strengths for the dominant methods upon which the extant body of knowledge has been built.

But those prescriptions still leave much room for choice. Often, there are several alternatives, all more or less equally distant, methodologically, from what has been done in the past. Each offers some (new) strengths but brings some (new) weaknesses as well. Thus, for example, for a problem for which past research has been dominated by the laboratory, either a field study, or a theoretical effort, or a sample survey, might provide substantial methodological distance from, and complements to the weaknesses of, the lab experiment—though each, of course, also brings its own characteristic weaknesses.

It is much easier to specify *what not to do next*. If one buys our fundamental premise that in research we seek convergence of substance among diverse and complementary methods, then the *worst* choice of method for the next step is clear: *Don't do what has been done* (i.e., the dominant method on that problem).

The striking fact, however, is that broadly, throughout social and behavioral science (and at *all* levels of strategy, design, and measurement), *we characteristically use in our next step, the very methods that we and others have used before on the same problem.* In fact, it is clear that one of the ways that a new research topic becomes prominent (a fad, if you will) is because someone presents an attractive and manageable paradigm for its study. The rapid rise to prominence of such topics as the risky shift, coalition formation, the two-person dilemma game, and communication nets, illustrates how interest in a topic expands, in part, because the next research study can use the already established (i.e., "approved") paradigm. But each of these topics also peaked and fell rapidly from fashion—in part, we would maintain, because they did not have diversity of methods (whether or not they had convergence of findings). The triangulations all put their observation posts in the same place!

Such paradigm-parroting is not the exception; rather, it is the rule for the social and behavioral sciences. Indeed, it is strongly supported in the unwritten norms of that scientific community, especially in regard to graduate students' training. How do you do research on risky shift? You start with the Choice Dilemma Questionnaire. How do you do research on communication in groups? You set up one or several of the standard communication nets. How do you study coalitions? Use the Vinacke/Arkoff coalition game.

This does not bespeak stupidity, or arbitrariness, on the part of those researchers and educators. There are some sound reasons for using extant "technology." On the practical side, it helps minimize development time and cost, which is especially important for the student trying to execute a dissertation. On the methodological side, it helps attain standardization, hence comparability over studies (but, see McGrath's chapter on the standardization-generalizability dilemma). Furthermore, and this applies especially for students doing dissertations, to use what has already been used (and is thus "established" in the journals), bestows legitimacy on the study in question.

What we are proposing here is in sharp contradiction to those norms. We suggest that the *worst* method for a next step on a problem is any method that has been heavily used in all or most prior studies on that problem. By so arguing, we are suggesting that *most* current social and behavioral science research has made precisely the worst possible choices of methods. *We have all been driving our triangulation posts into the self-same spot*!

What then about the much tauted, though seldom practiced, matter of replication? Is that not a desideratum in research? Certainly it is. It has its place, and it is essential in that place. But replication is complementary to, not a substitute for, generalizability/diversity/robustness. When a "finding" has been asserted (presumably on the basis of probabilistic-contingent-induction), we need replication—in the sense of a repetition of the same methods on the same problem—to decide whether to accept that assertion. In effect, it helps us decide whether to keep that asserted, probabilistic-contingent finding *in* the accumulating "body of knowledge." Results of a replication can either "confirm" or "disconfirm" what we already know—giving us more or less confidence in that specific, asserted finding. It cannot *add to* what we know, in the sense of new substantive information. Furthermore, it cannot add to the accumulation of "convergent knowledge from diverse methods," since the "new" evidence is contingent on the same methodological limits and weaknesses as was the prior evidence that it replicates. Results of a replication represent information about the reliability of a finding. To attain convergent or construct validity requires diversity of methods. To establish robustness or generalizability (external or discriminant validity) requires diversity of populations, occasions, and settings, as well as diversity of methods of study.

So we should, by all means, replicate each specific finding, lest our "body of knowledge" become highly polluted with many type I errors. But we must then establish the *meaning* of those findings by seeking convergence on them, via diverse, not redundant, methods.

MULTIPLE METHODS AND THE SINGLE RESEARCHER

Much of what we have said in this chapter, and in the three preceding ones, might seem to imply that every researcher must become knowledgeable about, and facile in, the use of *all possible* methods, at all levels (i.e., all strategies, all techniques for measurement, and so forth). We do not intend to imply that each researcher must be such an omnimethodologist. We would argue that each should be to some degree a multimethod person, at each level. That does not seem too much to ask of professionals, especially when we note that some of the methods and quasi-methods involve such matters as "read," "think," "know the literature in your problem area," and "talk to colleagues." But we very explicitly *do not* suggest that anyone ought to be expected to know, thoroughly, much less to practice, *all* the methods at all levels of the research enterprise.

We can discuss this matter by borrowing some metaphors from religions. We have asserted that no method is very good, but each method has some potential benefits. That is not unlike religion's dual prescriptions, that all humans are sinners, but all have some virtues worthy of efforts toward redemption. In that regard, we take an ecumenical view of methods. Every researcher should be able to *appreciate* the potential value of all methods—though recognizing the inherent flaws of each.

But by no means should each researcher try to use all methods in his or her own research. For one thing, any one researcher is unlikely to have resources to do so. Who among us has both a well-equipped lab and a survey organization at our disposal? Then, too, there is the matter of one's omni-method competence. Who among us is really skilled at all of the data-gathering techniques we know about, or all the data analysis techniques we have learned? To use the metaphor of religion again, any one researcher needs to be *catholic* in his or her appreciation of methods of all sorts, but *secular* in use of methods in his or her own work. What the individual researcher needs to do, toward the crucial goal of convergence-in-diversity, is *to get a patterned diversity of methods applied to his or her problem*—but not necessarily by him or her. It is often better, for reasons of competence and resources as already noted, to try to get someone else to apply radically different methods to the problem about which you are trying to accrue knowledge.

It is perhaps worth digressing to note that appreciation of a diversity of methods implies much more than just a passive tolerance for others when they use "different" methods. The ecumenical attitude here proposed requires an active effort to get to know and understand methods previously unfamiliar to you. Methods tend to develop as discipline-specific and even topic-specific tools. Hence, the ecumenical adventure here urged upon you requires reading in new problem areas, a change in beliefs and attitudes, and interdisciplinary orientation. Salvation does not come effortlessly!

The preceding discussion suggests that there are some other valuable roles involved in the total research enterprise, some of which we are want to overlook or undervalue. If the basic aim of the research enterprise is to get a diverse set of methods applied to a particular problem, and to get them applied by researchers who have the skills and available resources to apply them in a highly competent fashion, then we must regard as crucial to that enterprise sets of people who function in any of the following ways: (a) as *problem entrepreneurs*, whose role is to get resources and competent people committed to a given problem; (b) as *resource-brokers*, whose role is to provide important classes of resources for research; and (c) as *tool-jobbers*, whose role is to apply, with high technical competence, a particular subset of methods (e.g., tests, sample surveys, computer analyses) to any and all problems for which those methods can make a contribution. These are not fully research roles, nor are they substitutes for the classic role of the individual researcher. Rather, they are complementary to it. It is through these and other valuable "quasi-research" roles that many who work in research organizations, and many who serve as research sponsors and program expediters, make their very important contributions to the research enterprise.

We can return to the metaphors of religions to make one further point. Much discussion of methods in the social and behavioral sciences is carried out in evangelical tones, as if the participants were asserting that they had, methodologically speaking, the "one true faith." As a matter of fact, much of that discussion falls victim to what we will label "the curse of the false contrapositive." That line of discussion seems to argue: "if not X, then Y." For example, much of the methodological literature seems to say: "Your method, X, is flawed. *Therefore*, my method, Y, must be good." Several flaws in that line of argument will be apparent to the reader. First, for methods, X and Y seldom exhaust the universe of choices. Second, if X and Y are methods, then Y is flawed too, though differently than X. In any case, that syllogism is a non sequitur. It is relatively easy to detect and denote the flaws of the lab (or in the field study, in the survey, and so forth). Doing so does not thereby make some other method flawless.

Another example of methodological arguments involving inappropriate contrapositives would run as follows: "Since all methods are flawed, there is no 'one best method,' even for a given problem and set of research circumstances. If there is no 'right' method, then there is no 'wrong' method either. Hence, I can do anything I want to with equal (in)validity." This line of argument also has flaws, although they are not so glaring. While we would certainly agree that there is no "right" or "best" method, even for a given set of circumstances, there often are circumstances for which some particular set of methods are "poor" or "wrong," in the sense that they simply are not useful for gaining information in that situation. A certain method may only give a low-grade form of information of some specific kind. For example, you ought not use an opinion survey to determine how much two and two add up to. Or, as we have already pointed out, when a given method is the sole or main one used in past research on a problem, that method will not add much new information if it is used again.

So while it is possible to establish that a given method is poor, weak, limited, or flawed—in general or in a particular set of circumstances—it is not possible to establish that a certain method is "right" or "flawless" even for a particular situation. Moreover, it is certainly not logically sound to argue that the flawedness of one method implies the rightness of another. To return to the religious metaphor: We need methodological critics, and even skeptics, who point out the weaknesses of all of our methods; but *we do not need methodological evangelists, who allege or imply that their preferred methods constitute the one true faith.*

THE RESEARCHER AND THE RESEARCH ENTERPRISE

This broader view of the research enterprise can help us rationalize some anomalies of "research-as-practiced" compared to "research-as-idealized" that were brought out in the three preceding chapters. For example, those earlier chapters implied that the researcher's choices may be influenced by his or her purposes. You study what you study, and you make the choices that you make in your study, ultimately in large part because you have certain *purposes*. These purposes may arise from the requirements of your grant, from the implications of your theory, from your method competencies and preferences, from your publication needs, and even from your values, attitudes, and preferences as a human being. For far too long, social and behavioral scientists have argued about whether or not this ought to be the case. Here, we agree with the position taken by a number of scholars of the philosophy and sociology of social and behavioral science (e.g., Gergen, 1978; Horowitz, 1968; Ossowski, 1963; Stark, 1958) that such influence is inevitable, and is another inherent limitation of the Baconian paradigm. In our view, it is neither to be condoned nor condemned, but simply to be reckoned with. But it is extremely important, we believe, that you make explicit your purposes, and try to delineate their impact on your study—or at least that you do so to yourself.

On a more concrete level, Martin and Kulka make it clear that available resources, or preferred methods, often drive the choice of next step in research. In the "ecumenical" view presented here, that is as it should be—*provided* those researchers really could apply a rich and valuable set of resources, *provided* they were really competent in the preferred methods, and *provided*, above all, that the problem "needed" those resources and methods—that is, that those methods and resources represented an appreciable increment of "diversity of means."

Any one study can—indeed must—be method bound and resource and competence driven. But *all* studies in a given topic *must not* be narrowly method bound. Success of the research enterprise directed to a given problem is to be judged in terms of how well they, collectively, transcended resource and competence limitations to attain convergence of substance from diversity of methods. In contrast, success for the individual study is to be judged in terms of how well it did whatever it chose to do. We thus offer still another seeming paradox: *It is possible to do a study of a problem that is an excellent piece of research in its own terms but that makes utterly no contribution to the overall research enterprise bearing on the problem.* Not only is it possible; we submit that our field abounds with such studies.

Note, however, that we have shifted focus from the single researcher to the research enterprise. We have transformed the referent of our discussion, from "my research" or "my next study," to the "stream of intellectual material and activities" bearing on a given problem. We have transformed the basic aim of research, from "doing a sound study" or even "doing the best next study," to "making the maximum possible contribution to the extant body of knowledge" on that given problem. Moreover, we have transformed the "locus of responsibility," so to speak, from the individual researcher—what he or she can and must do, should and should not do, and the like—to the total collection of people (some researchers, some practitioners, some consumers perhaps) who have a stake in improving/ expanding the body of knowledge on a given problem. *We do not ask omnimethod competence of the single researcher— but we demand it of the collective.* At the same time, we ask the individual researcher to regard his or her own efforts less as "independent research," and more as his or her unique contribution to the collective research enterprise on that particular problem. It is through convergence of the efforts of diverse researchers, using diverse methods and playing diverse roles in the research enterprise, that we will make progress—if, indeed, we do. Such progress requires divergence of means, but it also requires some self-conscious coordination of our collective work.

REFERENCES

CAMPBELL, D. T. and D. W. FISKE (1959) "Convergent and discriminant valida-
   tion by the multitrait-multimethod matrix." Psychological Bulletin 56: 81-105.
GERGEN, K. J. (1978) "Toward generative theory." Journal of Personality and Social
   Psychology 36: 1344-1360.
HOROWITZ, I. L. (1968) Professing Sociology: Studies in the Life Cycle of Social
   Science. Chicago IL: Aldine.
OSSOWSKI, S. (1963) Class Structure in the Social Consciousness. New York:
   Macmillan.
STARK, W. (1958) The Sociology of Knowledge. London: Routledge & Kegan Paul.

5

Some Judgments on the Judgment Calls Approach

Barry M. Staw

☐ The chapters by Martin, Kulka, and McGrath each address what could be labeled as the "underbelly" of social research—those thoughts, actions, constraints, and choices that lurk beneath the surface of our well-dressed research publications. Each chapter addresses how social research deviates from the normative prescriptions of methodological texts and why even the most quantitative research is more qualitative than meets the eye. After completing these chapters, the reader should be more than ever convinced that the phrase, "the appropriate analysis is . . . " is indeed an inappropriate statement on research method.

In the first chapter, Joanne Martin describes methodological decisions in the same way that March and his colleagues have treated organizational decision making. Instead of the idealized or normatively rational procedures of science, Martin argues that the exercise of methodological choices may resemble a garbage can model of decision making (Cohen, March, and Olson, 1972; March and Olson, 1978). As Martin notes, research does not always follow the logical sequence of problem formulation, design, analysis, and interpretation that we learned from the textbooks. In contrast, the garbage can model of research notes that problems, resources, choice opportunities, and solutions all combine to produce a research product. She argues that recognition of this garbage can process can help us to identify overlooked problems and methods and can help us to train students in the "street smarts" necessary to do good research.

The Kulka chapter provides some of the "data" for the garbage can perspective on research. Through interviews and excerpts from published material, Kulka weaves a description of how the practice of research is conditioned by resources, sponsorship, prior training, and experience, as well as by a variety of opportunities and threats facing the researcher. The researcher is seen as having personal and institutional motives in choosing a particular research problem, and methodology is seen to result as much from situational constraints and habits as from the dictates of science.

If the Martin and Kulka chapters are not enough to frighten unjaded investigators, McGrath takes us a step further in that direction. Whereas Martin and Kulka have attempted to describe how research, as it actually gets done, deviates from the scientific model, McGrath questions that model in principle. McGrath argues that all studies are inherently flawed, even if they are well executed. This is because the methodological choices we make are not simply correct or incorrect on technical grounds but are attempts to resolve dilemmas inherent in the research process. Although there are existing "rules of thumb" and prevailing research orthodoxies, McGrath notes that there can be no logical solution to dilemmas such as precision versus generalizability, experimental versus correlational designs, and reliability versus validity. Because all research is inherently flawed, our only hope, as McGrath sees it, is to triangulate over studies, building knowledge over time through a series of imperfect studies.

COPING WITH UNCERTAINTY, OR
HOW TO BE A SANITARY ENGINEER

If the research act is really a garbage can process, how do investigators engineer a coping strategy? In my opinion, research is like other complex and messy problems, comprising multiple and conflicting criteria and frequently changing states of nature. Like other decisions of this sort, it is not feasible to survey all possible courses of action and to weigh the consequences of each. The process is too complex to come up with a computational answer, and such solutions will probably be wrong anyway since the opportunities and constraints facing the researcher are not obvious in advance. In the midst of such uncertainty, several strategies seem feasible.

Habit, Convention, and Rules of Thumb. When technical solutions are not clear, it is easy to see why social conventions and norms are formed. Since no one really knows what to do, experts are referenced (e.g., Campbell, Cronback, Winer), precedents are followed (e.g., "as in previous work on this topic"), and practices become legitimated (e.g., the assumption of interval scales where even ordinal may be suspect). Because only some of these conventions become codified into written rules (probably the most obvious and defensible), there arises the need for what Martin refers to as "street smarts" and for the informal exchange of war stories and experiences. Without such jaded wisdom, even a thorough reading of all major texts on methodology and statistics will not seriously reduce the uncertainty of the research process.

Placing Action Ahead of Thought. When the parameters of a problem cannot be anticipated and when states of nature change frequently, it is often preferable to charge into the problem rather than try to outflank it. Connolly (1980) describes these types of problems as similar to hedgeclipping (where you make adjustments as you go), or insulating an attic (where you should buy a lot and start unrolling since calculations will always be in error). Lindblom (1959) similarly prescribes a "science of muddling through," and Campbell (1969), a program of experimentation for cases in which it is useful to do something but that "something" should be molded to the parameters of the situation as they unfold. Thus, a successful researcher is often one who (like a policymaker) is able to make quick adjustments of a design as circumstances warrant and who does not easily burn his or her methodological bridges.

An Informed Retreat from Idealism. Another useful strategy for research is to recognize the full utility of the normative model, but to retreat from it gracefully and intelligently. An idealized model of research can be drawn up so as to determine what type of design would be preferred. Then, as constraints are brought to mind, one might try to identify the sacrifices that occur in dealing with research realities. Although many design problems cannot be anticipated, some of the deepest pitfalls can be negotiated by making intelligent trade-off decisions. For example, a retreat from true experimentation can be made with full awareness of the attendant threats to validity, while the reduction of variables, measures, and samples will understandably limit construct validity, reliability, and generalizability. The astute researcher may thus be one who zealously guards those aspects of the design that are central to the contribution or impact of a study, while feeding smaller game to the surrounding predators.

Mocking Out a Design. A final way in which an individual researcher might cope with the uncertainties of design could resemble the architectural planning process. The investigator may have a rough vision or purpose in choosing a research question (e.g., to demonstrate a particular effect, understand a process, refute a colleague), but is not wedded to a particular methodology. By keeping one's purpose squarely in mind, different models can be constructed, revised, and rejected until something acceptable seems to appear. Of course, the problem with this procedure is that one must simulate the path of the research in order to shape a reasonable model. Working out two or more models in advance should facilitate good research, but it obviously does not guarantee it. Remember that although an architect can work on both the details and overall purpose of a model, the materials to be used have known properties and the technology of construction is well established. The astute researcher, on the other hand, must make do with a limited set of experiences and fertile imagination in order to construct a realistic model of the planned investigation

These are but a few of the strategies that an individual might use to cope with the messy problem that we call research. The garbage can process that both Martin and Kulka describe is the way research decisions look to the observer, since they neither fit the textbook descriptions nor conform closely to an alternative model. However, there is, I am sure, a logic that describes the individual's research actions that is more precise than the random flow of the garbage can. There are also, I am sure, some useful coping strategies that have never been codified by research methodologists. Therefore, let us not be as shocked by departures from the normative model as we are excited by the informal solutions worked out and practiced by researchers. Some recording and transfer of this expertise is a logical next step to the work of Martin, Kulka, and McGrath.

SOME NOTES ON THE RESEARCH ENTERPRISE

Because of the inherent shortcomings of any given study, Martin, Kulka, and McGrath stress the need for triangulation of research. They note that one should not be apologetic about the poor generalizability of lab studies or weak causal inference from surveys, but should instead push each method to its own maximum strengths. They also note that it is probably better for different people to triangulate on a topic than it is for researchers to attempt to use methodologies with which they are less familiar and skilled.

Because it is difficult to disagree with the plea for triangulation, one must wonder why we do not do more of it. As McGrath, Martin, and Kulka note, someone frequently finds a way to measure an interesting phenomena (e.g., risk taking) and then we are swamped with monomethod research. Likewise, once an experimental treatment has successfully tested a theoretical process (e.g., the counterattitudinal advocacy paradigm in dissonance research), we may see hundreds of studies that vary only slightly from the prototype. How can we explain this pattern of activity?

One reason we largely replicate, rather than triangulate, relates to the uncertainty of the research process. The need for legitimacy and acceptance of a given procedure runs high when uncertainty is pervasive and demands for publication are great. Also, because a series of studies (even using a single method) will usually uncover conflicting and moderated relationships, there is real motivation to finish the small (monomethod) problem before opening a multimethod can of worms. Finally, because social phenomena are often difficult to isolate, let alone replicate, any procedure that does reliably produce an effect is ripe for repeated study. Once a procedure is developed that "grows the appropriate culture," few researchers are willing to start again with an unknown set of procedures.

What commonly breaks the monomethod lock on methodology is the disillusionment that accompanies real progress in understanding a problem in its most trivial or limited form. Having understood, at last, why counterattitudinal advocacy studies work does not, for example, speak loudly to the condition of mankind or important forms of behavior. Therefore, an entire area of study may wither before it has ever broadened, or (more fortunately) get subsumed under another theoretical umbrella.

As structural solutions to the problem, one can think of ways to facilitate triangulation but none that will ensure it. First and foremost, literature reviews should array the data on a given topic by research method or threat to validity, graphically displaying the voids in prior research and the common sources of invalidity found in prior work. Such a model has already been provided by Salipanti, Notz, and Bigelow (forthcoming), and it holds promise in publicizing and legitimizing needed triangulation. Unfortunately, working against this model is the recent popularity of various forms of meta-analysis (Glass, 1977; Schmidt and Hunter, 1977). Meta-analysis simply accumulates the evidence; it does not weigh it by the breadth of methodology addressing the issue.

Other structural solutions to triangulation draw on Martin, Kulka, and McGrath's roles for the researcher as problem entrepreneurs, resource-brokers, and tool-jobbers. Because researchers who have developed the leading method to address a problem are also thrust into leading academic roles, these individuals are often in a position of power to encourage or discourage triangulation. In their roles as gatekeepers and summarizers of evidence on their old topic areas, these "method founders" can have enormous leverage on what new research gets done. If such exhortations do fail, however, the founder can attempt to do the triangulating himself or herself. Although such practice ignores Martin, Kulka, and McGrath's advice, we might assume that any seriously flawed efforts at triangulation will produce a welcome storm of protest and a set of competing studies.

Finally, in proposing structural solutions, we must keep in mind the size and time period over which the research enterprise is envisioned. While Martin, Kulka, and McGrath assume scores of researchers either triangulating or monomethoding a multitude of problems, the research community is probably thinner than they suggest. Other than the most eye-catching examples (e.g., dissonance, risky-shift, attribution theory), many topics get researched by a very few people and over a relatively short time period. In such cases, the method and idea founder must triangulate or no one else will. The founder may also resort to mixed research strategies (e.g., a realistic experiment, a survey with longitudinal components, and other variants not discussed by these authors), when the problem is socially important yet time and resources prohibit a fully flanked attack. Work on applied and fleeting problems may thereby not receive nor deserve the full triangulation suggested for core, academic problems.

CONCLUSION

What Martin, Kulka, and McGrath have contributed in these chapters is a brew that is realistic, disturbing, and, at the same time, hopeful. They force us to recognize what we are, and as researchers this is disturbing. Yet, they do provide means for arranging our weaknesses into strengths, and they describe some important guides for the entire research enterprise. Although I have added some footnotes and modifications to their ideas, I certainly concur with their general analyses and conclusions. Martin, Kulka, and McGrath have offered us sound advice and we should take it.

REFERENCES

CAMPBELL, D. T. (1969) "Reforms as experiments." American Psychologist 24: 409-429.

COHEN, M. D., J. G. MARCH, and J. P. OLSEN (1972) "A garbage can model of organizational choice." Administrative Science Quarterly 17: 1-25.

CONNOLLY, T. (1980) "Uncertainty, action and competence" in S. Fiddle (ed.) Uncertainty: Behavioral and Social Dimensions. New York: Praeger.

GLASS, G. V (1977) "Integrating findings: the meta-analysis of research." Review of Research in Education 5: 351-379.

LINDBLOM, C. E. (1959) "The science of muddling through." Public Administration Review 19: 79-88.

MARCH, J. G. and J. P. OLSEN (1976) Ambiguity and Choice in Organizations. Bergen, Norway: Universitels Forlaget.

SALIPANTI, P., W. NOTZ and J. BIGELOW (forthcoming) "A matrix approach to literature reviews," in B. Staw and L. Cummings (eds.) Research in Organizational Behavior (Vol. 4). Greenwich, CT: JAI Press.

SCHMIDT, F. L. and J. E. HUNTER (1977) "Development of a general solution to the problem of validity generalization." Journal of Applied Psychology 62: 529-540.

About the Authors

JOSEPH E. McGRATH is Professor of Psychology at the University of Illinois, Urbana. He has authored or coauthored a number of books and articles on small group research, stress, and research methodology. He is the editor of the *Journal of Social Issues,* the official publication of the Society for the Psychological Study of Social Issues.

JOANNE MARTIN is Associate Professor of Organizational Behavior (and of Sociology) at the Stanford Graduate School of Business. She has published studies of relative deprivation and perceived injustice, and of scripts, stories and legends in organization.

RICHARD A. KULKA is a research specialist at the Research Triangle Institute. He has authored or coauthored a number of books and articles on mental health, and on using survey methodology for studying change.

BARRY M. STAW is Professor of Organizational Behavior at the School of Business Administration, University of California, Berkeley. His main areas of research are individual commitment, motivations, and decision making in organizations.